**Just A Dad
Fighting For My Kids**

ROBERT CURTIS ANDERSON

**MISSION
POSSIBLE
PRESS**

Creating Legacies through Absolute Good Works

The Mission is Possible.

Sharing love and wisdom for the young and "the young at heart," expanding minds, restoring kindness through good thoughts, feelings, and attitudes is our intent. May you thrive and be good in all you are and all you do...

Be Cause U.R. Absolute Good!

To Hell And Back, Just A Dad Fighting For My Kids
© 2019 Robert Curtis Anderson

No part of this book may be reproduced in any written, electronic, recording, or photocopying form without written permission of the publisher. The exception would be in the case of brief quotations embodied in critical articles or reviews and pages where permission is specifically granted by the publisher.

Although every precaution has been taken to verify the accuracy of the information contained herein, the author and publisher assume no responsibility for any errors or omissions. No liability is assumed for damages that may result from the use of information contained within. All rights reserved worldwide.

Books may be purchased in quantity by contacting the publisher directly:

Mission Possible Press, A division of Absolute Good

PO Box 8039 St. Louis, MO 63156

or by calling 240.644.2500

MissionPossiblePress.com

ISBN: 978-0-9996766-3-9

First Edition   Printed in the United States

Dedication

I dedicate this book to my parents, who taught me to persevere.

To my sister who has been my rock.

And to my children for being the reason I do so.

Acknowledgments

To my best friend, the late Rob Audette, who was like the big brother I never had. To my cousin, the late Jimmie Chamberlain, who was like the little brother I never had, who though he never got the chance to be a biological parent, through his guidance and help I was able to raise my children, with him covering my bases many times, and who was a father figure to them. You both changed me for the better.

To Wayne H., who has been like a second father to me. Without his guidance I'm not sure that my fight for my children would have been successful. Thank you brother.

Thanks to the mothers of my children for the gift of them, and to my former mate for dedicating a significant part of her life to helping raise them. Through each of them, we experienced love, parenthood and the ultimate gift of shaping the lives of innocent souls. I do believe they gave their best, and for that, I'm grateful.

Thanks to Nana, for taking on the grandmother role to my little ones when we all needed you.

Thanks to my writing coach and publisher Jo Lena Johnson for guiding me through uncharted waters during such a tumultuous time, resulting in this work.

Contents

Dear Dads 1
A Taste of Fatherhood 3
Fatherhood and Child Support 7
My Father's Influence 13
Protecting My Children Took Almost Everything I Had 19
My Buddy and the Bank 23
Fighting for My Kids 33
Single Dad 39
About Therapy 47
Navigating the Custody Battle 51
Becky Transformed Our Lives 59
The Shift 65
A Gun Down the Throat 71
Battles in Our Home 75
Fleeing Tucson 85
Manning Up 93
Black Family 99
Environment and Circumstances Shape Children 105
Don't Use the Kids to Hurt the Other Parent 111
My Top 7 Responsibilities When Rearing Children,
Especially as a Black Father 115
Building Healthy Relationships in the Aftermath 117
Resources for Fathers 119
About the Author 121

"It takes a man half his life to learn how to live it."

– My dad, Robert Curtis Anderson, Sr.,

Dear Dads

I feel emotional, a lot more than I thought I would be. Thinking of the losses, and the things my kids and I went through, brings up a myriad of emotions. It's harder than I thought it would be to share my feelings in addition to the stories however, persevere, I must. Emotionally, I knew I needed to be open and truthful so that you, as the reader can understand the difficulties of being a man and a father.

Tired of being all over the place, I'm ready for a change. Questioning myself about making decisions about the children, and for myself, as it comes to moving forward with them, with me, and in future relationships. It's been a difficult journey. At times, I've pulled on the side of the road and just cried. I've cried about the violence, the manipulation, the things my children witnessed and the pain they felt at seeing us treated poorly by people who said they loved us. It's surely changed the way we see life and ourselves.

Overexposure, especially when children are little, is a terrible thing, and can make growing up and maturing more difficult, especially in this world of technology, video games, violence and bitterness. Writing this book and getting in touch with the things which occurred in the past has been a healthy dose of therapy of sorts, and it's also been a solid start for the building of our future, our, meaning my teenaged children and me, their middle-aged dad. As I share some of the stories, I'm doing my best to share the thoughts and emotions behind them, but also know, that as a man, it's difficult. If you are a man reading this, you know what I'm saying.

Just stay strong brothers, and don't try doing it on your own. Support, along with faith, prayer and surrounding yourself with trustworthy people who have your best interests at heart is crucial. Don't fight that – being healthy is something you deserve. Don't be afraid to question the past, but also, take the lessons from it and choose to move forward. It's a daily process, but it's worth it because your kids need a healthy dad, at the very least.

Well, let's get to it.

Rob

A Taste of Fatherhood

Prior to becoming a father at 23, I was immature in certain ways, independent and reckless behind the wheel. I had several driving infractions – including speeding, improper lane changes and driving without insurance. As a result, I had an SR22, high risk insurance, which meant that I had to pay my premiums six months in advance. Had I gone to college, I would have become a Game Warden, however, I didn't continue my education so, faced with being a young, undereducated father, I had to do something to stabilize my life. After Allison was born I straightened up. My first daughter's birth gave me the push I needed to grow up and become a responsible man and father. But you'll see that my choices in relationships really dictated many of the challenges I, and ultimately, my children faced.

I wasn't afforded the option of "full-time dad" with Allison. Losing the chance to raise my baby girl did something to me. And I promised myself that should I have any other children, I would raise them, no matter what.

My own dad, Robert Curtis Anderson, Sr. used to tell me, "It takes a man half his life to learn how to live it." At nearly 50 years old, I have to agree with him. Being removed from the situations now, I'm able to see things more clearly. However, in the middle, I was drowning. If you or someone you know is living in the eye of the storm, hold on.

I'm moving forward and hoping to push, pull, support and encourage other men, dads and especially our sons. As men, we don't often talk about what's on our minds or in our hearts, especially when it comes to pain and feelings, however, if we did more of it, perhaps we would be healthier and ultimately better men and fathers.

Overcome Injustice and Bitterness

There are so many dads out there like me. And so many children that also experience the ill effects of an unjust system – because of the injustices towards the dads. We are also affected by the women who keep our kids from us if they become bitter due to things not working out. What I've learned and what you'll hear in my story is also how bitterness can turn into vengefulness. Therefore, the importance staying strong while also creating an emotional support system is astronomical.

Don't try to do everything by yourself. You need a team of family, friends and professionals to help you navigate the system, know your rights, listen during the tough times, encourage you when you want to give up, feed you when you're broke and hold you up when you feel too weak to stand.

Everything you do matters. You might be tempted to ride the wave, throw your hands up and go where the system takes you. However, you have to stay, for the long haul. It matters – the kids will remember and they will validate what you do. It's important for you, at all costs, to remain vigilant.

As fathers we must learn the skills and have the tools and information necessary for each child, and find it within ourselves to do what it takes to create a healthy environment, and to also maintain it.

Necessary Information You Need to Know

- Birth Date
- Hospital where child was born
- Social Security Number
- The pediatrician – build and maintain a relationship, along with open communication with him/her.
- The school – build a relationship with administration and teachers, and be actively involved.
- Insure you are on all medical and school records as a contact.
- Create a contact list in the event of an emergency.

Lack of involvement comes at a price. Being involved will save you time and money because the mother is not going to share much when you are at odds. If you are filing for custody, or you are concerned about the well-being of your children, knowing the intricate details of their life is important for all parties, including the court system.

If you find yourself in a damaging situation with your children, your saving grace is therapy. Documentation, documentation, documentation! I can't stress that enough.

And about therapy, I realize many of us, especially as Black people/men don't ascribe to therapy, but it's designed to support, especially when you find someone who is a good fit. Please don't shy away from it – for your children and for you.

"Even if you made mistakes yesterday, take action today. Your children need you."

Fatherhood and Child Support

"If you don't handle your business through the courts, you can end up in jail for child support."

When I was 23 years old, my first daughter, Allison, was born in Greenwood, Mississippi. I was dating her mother Diana for about a year when she became pregnant. We were both living in Atlanta, but Diana was from Greenwood. Though it was unplanned, we were happy about the prospect of becoming parents. During the pregnancy, I found out she was cheating on me. I had verifiable proof but I won't go into the gory details, out of respect for our youthful ages at the time and our daughter. I was committed to being a provider but I also felt angry, confused and in denial.

During the pregnancy I wondered if the baby she was carrying was even my child. I did love her, yet I also stayed with her because if that child was mine, I definitely wanted to raise her. I spent the rest of the pregnancy back in Salt Lake City, where I had spent my formative years, looking for career opportunities and doing my best to get over my hurt. I had a one-way airline ticket scheduled for her due date however, Allison arrived early. I flew to Atlanta and caught a bus to Greenwood.

The first time we laid eyes on Allison, my whole family knew she was mine. I fell in love with her the moment I saw her. It was the happiest day of my life. We had an immediate bond. An adorable bundle of joy, at that moment I knew had to I get some steady income, a stable career with benefits, to take care of my family.

Baby Carriage and Marriage?

Now that we were a family unit, Diana put the pressure on for us to get married. Though I said I was willing to go ahead with the ceremony, the night before I changed my mind. I thought I could get past the cheating and mistrust but I could not. I literally got on the bus in Mississippi and left her at the altar. It was the wrong thing to do. I was young and immature about it. Instead of telling her how I felt, like a man, I was angry and hurt and felt leaving was better than dealing with the situation. As a result, she was upset and embarrassed, vowing to never let me see my child again.

The first couple of months were difficult. Diana was angry and I was focused on getting gainful employment. I decided that I was going to be a FedEx tractor trailer driver because that's where the "good money" was going to be for someone in my position. I was told they would never hire me because of my driving history. However, I wanted to do it and was determined. In order to achieve my goal, I had some work to do. I laid out a plan to get my driving record cleaned up so that I could become a driver and have access to the money I wanted for my child. When I got the call from FedEx offering me a job, I was relieved that I was starting a career.

Diana held Allison from me for a while but eventually allowed us time. Thankfully, she brought Allison to my parents' home to visit, and I got a chance to spend time with my baby. That's when we began to bond and create a relationship.

Child Support

With my part-time job I wasn't able to give Diana a lot of money for Allison's child support. Yet, I gave her what I had, and paid her regularly. At the end of the year she wanted more than I was giving her. When I got my income tax return, I got about $2,000 back and gave her approximately $700. It wasn't enough for her, she wanted more. I told her I wasn't giving her more. She told me she would file child support charges on me. I told her to do what she had to do. She did.

About a month later the Sherriff's Department sent a couple of units to my parents' house but I wasn't there. When I got there, they informed me that Cobb County had a warrant out for my arrest for child support. I, having been taught to abide by the law, went to the police station with my receipts in hand. The majority of child support I had given her was in cash and then in money orders. I showed the officers my receipts and they told me I would have to be placed under arrest and wait until I could see the judge.

I was in jail for two days, with child support receipts in my pocket. When I saw the judge he said that he could tell I had been paying, however he had to find me guilty because it wasn't through the court system. He said that being on child support would benefit me in the long run because I'd be able to show, in black and white, my payments and that the court would keep track.

Being in jail was one of the most degrading experiences I ever had and I vowed I would do everything in my power to keep from being in that position again.

Actions Have Consequences

Had I spoken honestly, in the beginning that would have alleviated some of the drama and problems between Diana and me. I should have told her I didn't trust or believe her, and because of that, I wasn't going to marry her. That would have saved a lot of embarrassment and hard feelings for both of us.

Because I chose to take the bus instead of going to the altar, those actions had long term consequences which affected our ability to communicate, co-parent, and also affected the way my daughter's mother spoke about me, her father. I lost a lot of quality time with my daughter during important events in her life. Thankfully, despite the issues Diana and I had, she was a college-educated woman with a great career and been a good mother to Allison, along with her (now-deceased) husband, who my daughter adored.

Allison's stepfather and I ultimately got along. I was thankful for him because we had a good understanding, as we met on a couple of occasions, just the two of us, allowing us to get to know each other and to agree to communicate when necessary, all in the best interest of Allison. When conflicts happened during the course of raising our child/teenager, we checked each other. We both loved them and both had a responsibility to respect them and each other. We chose to work through the difficulties because it was in the best interest of Allison. Our communication helped us to be more mature men who learned to work together for the good of family.

> *"What happened when my first child was born taught me maturity. When her stepfather came into the picture, he helped to bridge gaps her mother and I couldn't. There's no formula to fatherhood but putting the child first is what we have to do, no matter what."*

"Find a way, make a way, no matter what."
- My dad, Robert Curtis Anderson, Sr.,

My Father's Influence

"My parents were married until my dad passed in mom's arms. I wanted love like theirs."

My parents had a unique life-long relationship. My dad was a nomad and gypsy and my mother loved him and loved the life she had with him. It's as if they were made for each other. I learned about family, sacrifice and commitment through them. I have prayed for a relationship like they had. It hasn't happened for me, at least not yet, but I haven't thrown in the towel.

My Foundation Influenced My Future

My grandparents raised my mom and her four sisters in a Catholic home in St. Louis, Missouri, where they attended parochial schools. My parents met when mom was 14 years old. Because her parents felt they were too young to date, my dad pretended to like one of her older sisters so that he would be allowed to hang around until he could get close enough to let his intentions be known.

My grandfather didn't like my dad because he was from a rough area and felt he wasn't good enough for his daughter. Eventually, that changed and he was loved and adored by both of my grandparents.

My dad was born in Caruthersville, and was raised in St. Louis; he was the youngest of four sisters and a brother. He started playing pool when he was 11 or 12, taking his lunch money to go gamble. He quickly realized his ability to earn a decent amount of money for a kid his age, and always had money because of that. He attended Vashon High School. He started smoking weed in his freshman year and continued throughout his life. He eventually developed a hard core drug habit, from which he never completely recovered.

Dad served in Vietnam as an Army Ranger and Paratrooper, and was awarded the Purple Heart, for saving the lives of his fellow servicemen at the age of 18 years old. After serving his term he returned to St. Louis and was diagnosed as having Post-Traumatic Stress Disorder (PTSD). He married my mom and I was born, then my sister.

Dad became a professional billiards player. It was his passion, he was highly skilled, and because he had a hard time holding down regular jobs, dealing with authority, related to the PTSD, he played pool for long stretches of time to support his family. To supplement his income, he worked for General Electric and the Better Business Bureau; and as a car salesman, and radio DJ on a country music station, throughout the years.

Dad Always Had A Plan, Sort Of

I remember going to the recycling centers, scrapping metal to earn money with my dad. He was a hustler to the core. That was one of the main things I got from him, "Find a way, make a way, no matter what." He had a strong work-ethic and knew from experience that money, a good education and a safe, family-friendly environment were important factors in child-rearing. When I was 11 years old, Dad didn't feel raising his Black son in St. Louis was in my best interest so he packed up our family and we left.

We headed to Alaska, in our station wagon, where my dad was planning to get work in the lucrative job market. On our way, the car broke down in Wyoming. We were out of money so he played pool to earn enough to continue the trip. It took a few months to get us back on the road. We continued our journey and broke down again in Salt Lake City, Utah. While there, he played pool, got a job and so did my mom. It was going pretty well so they decided to stay.

My parents enrolled my sister and me in private schools. Dad always encouraged us to learn and found unconventional ways to give us incentives. For example, instead of giving us an allowance, he paid us to read, giving us $1.50 per paperback and $2.00 per hardcover. My sister always had money and graduated from a great private school, Judge Memorial. I on the other hand, wanted to play football, didn't have good study habits and eventually graduated from a public school, because of my own choices. We lived in Utah until I was 19. After my sister graduated, our family moved to Atlanta for better opportunities, as we had heard it was a good job market for African Americans.

Atlanta

Once we got to Atlanta my dad's drug habit got worse because he was hustling a lot more, and the high-stakes pool circuit was much more cut-throat. My sister took a job with an international airline. My mother established a career, with FedEx, through which she retired. I had miscellaneous jobs to that point, headed nowhere fast. Diana and I dated for a couple of years, and then she gave birth do our daughter. I got serious and asked Mom to help me get hired at FedEx, and that's how my career started.

As a part-time package handler I earned $7.80 an hour, with excellent benefits. I had to start in that position in order to reach my ultimate goal, tractor trailer driving. I've been working for FedEx for over 25 years.

We all lived in Atlanta for six years until I was transferred for my dream position in Vermont. Once I arrived, ready to drive tractor trailers, we discovered a glitch in my contract which prevented me from full-time driving until all of those traffic infractions from Atlanta fell off my record. That meant nearly three years of working as a part-time handler/courier, with less pay and different duties. I had to maintain my living situation and had child support to pay. Because of that I needed my parents support in order to survive. In August of 1995 without question, they packed up their lives and moved to Vermont to keep me from sinking.

Leaving Atlanta helped my dad get away from the fast living. He got a lot better. About three years later we all returned home to St. Louis, following my job transfer. They bought a house, settled in and were doing well for a few years, and then Dad's habit started getting out of control again. My father was never able to fully commit to anything because of his progressive drug problem. He traveled around the country for pool tournaments and would leave for a week or three at a time, with varying levels of financial success. As he got older he made less and less money though a few times he "hit big."

Prior to my father's passing, he became sober for several months. We thought he was in the clear, and then he relapsed. Had it not been for my mother, he likely would have died years ago.

My father, Robert, Sr. transitioned in the arms of my mother in January of 2012.

Living and Leading Children

Dad was a daredevil and defied so many odds, despite his addiction. When I was 18 years old he revealed that the first time he tried heroin was when he was 13 years old. Hearing that was mortifying, to me. I didn't even know what heroin was at the time and found it hard to believe that "back then" he was exposed to something so potent at such a young age. I think he told me that so that I would always reconsider if I thought of doing drugs, not wanting me to follow his example. That conversation helped to shape the way I saw him, his habit and my own choices about drugs and alcohol. Though I tried weed a few times, I didn't like the feeling and vowed not to smoke it again. I haven't. Around the time my daughter was born, I wanted to prove to my dad that it's possible not to indulge, so I went 15 years without consuming alcohol. I'd like to think I influenced him, as he had several periods of sobriety during that period.

Despite the addiction, I think highly of my father and his intelligence. I credit him and my mother for giving me a solid respect for family and a strong commitment to being a dedicated father. He developed in me the mindset that anything is attainable.

> *"Dad always said, 'The sky is the limit and the stars are opportunities, you just have to pick one.'"*

Protecting My Children Took Almost Everything I Had

"Taking responsibility means changing what's not working."

I met Frances in 2001, she had two sons who were eight and six at the time. We got married and Joseph was born in 2003 and then Angelina two years later. Our marriage was wonderful in the beginning. I did everything in my power to make her happy. About a month after Joseph was born, there was a microburst (small tornado) that came through the small Arizona town, where we lived, and tore the roof off of the house we were renting. We were offered another rental opportunity but after the first experience, I didn't want to do that again.

I had made up my mind that I wasn't renting from anybody else and wanted to raise our children in my own house. It was difficult to stay in the Motel 6 with our three sons for the couple of months it took for me to find a house for us, but the motel was two miles from my job so that part was easy. I was looking for something that was affordable, nice and close to my job. I knew what I wanted so it took time to find that and close on it.

Joseph was three months old when we moved into the house. We got the boys into school and everything was going well. Once Angelina was born, things started turning into a nightmare. It was a host of things which contributed to our demise. I found out more about Frances' past and I also think her hormones were affected when she got pregnant again, after Angelina, having three pregnancies so close together.

Things Started Blowing Up

I found out that Frances had been molested as a child for many years by her uncle, her mother's brother, and then became a practicing lesbian for years after that, before meeting me. Things got so out of control that she was arrested in 2005 and twice in 2006 for domestic violence against me, with the kids present each time. It was horrifying. I think me finding out her secrets was too much for her to handle. Once I knew, in her mind, she was afraid I would never look at her the same. She felt it was something she and I couldn't get over. I believe she subconsciously sabotaged our marriage. I could've and would've gotten over all of those things had we just continued on with our lives. But in her mind, and to this day, she takes no responsibility for the demise of our relationship or for her need for help.

It's almost inconceivable to think that a mother would not naturally want to nurture and protect her children. Sometimes that's the case. It's important to put the children's best interests first, regardless of the heart, feelings or circumstances. I've done my best over the years yet it was never easy. I learned a lot through the process. It was especially difficult when I had to respond in the moment to foolishness, insults, dangerous situations and dire straits as a result of their mother's influence and behavior. It also became increasingly difficult to pay for needed intervention. It worked out in the end, but the journey was taxing.

"My grandmother said, 'A good woman is worth her weight in gold for a man, so choose wisely.'"

My Buddy and the Bank

My good friend Willis was instrumental in giving me advice and supporting me as my marriage was breaking up. He was a Vietnam Vet, and old enough to be my dad. He had gone through several marriages and divorces, with children. Willis had lost houses, money, custody and everything else you can imagine, so he had endless amounts of knowledge from which I benefitted. I'm grateful to Willis for being a sounding board and confidant.

Toward the end of my marriage Willis admitted that he hadn't liked Frances ever, from day one. He said he could tell I was mesmerized by her ass and that it would do nothing but ruin our friendship if he said something to me.

When I moved out of the house, Willis allowed me to stay in a spare room in his home. I was missing my kids and wanted my family to be together.

One morning after getting off at 7 a.m., I drove around the city, despite being exhausted. I saw a Baptist church and went inside, where a group of people were sitting and sharing their issues and problems. I'm Catholic and knew nothing about what they were doing. I talked and cried harder than I ever had in my life, on my knees in a foyer, in front of all of those people. I didn't care who saw me in that big group of strangers, mainly women. With two women rubbing my head and trying to comfort me I sobbed, "I love my wife, I want to be with my wife." It was the greatest pain I had ever experienced. I prayed, asking God how He was going to get me past that. It took me years, with baby steps.

Frances baited me into coming back to the house even though she had filed a restraining order against me due to an altercation we had a month earlier. She asked me to come to the house on that Thursday and assured me that on Monday we would go to the courthouse and get the restraining order lifted.

When I told Willis I was going back home he said, "Rob, are you sure?"

I said, "Yes." He was hesitant to see me go but I was determined to be with my family. I repacked all of my stuff and headed home.

Back at the House

I was happy to be back with my family and the kids were happy as well. Frances was six months pregnant. I believed we would work things out. The kids were asleep. I was worn out from having moved my things back into the house. We had settled down for the night. I turned off the lamp around 1 a.m., closed my eyes, and all of a sudden felt a tap on my chest.

Frances said, "And by the way, I don't want Willis coming by the house again. I don't want you calling him anymore. And I don't want you all to be friends anymore."

I said, "Excuse me? Why are you telling me this now, this late in the night? And since when do you tell me who I can and can't be friends with? I'm a grown ass man."

At that point, she reached over me and turned on her bedside lamp. "Okay, get your shit and get out right now. Get out."

My back was hurting from moving in. I was tired, exhausted actually. When I moved back in, one thing I did right, which saved my ass, instead of hanging my keys on the key ring next to the front door, I put them in our bathroom drawer. I normally would have hung the keys and put my wallet on the nightstand. I had put them in the bathroom drawer. I had doubt back in the recesses of my mind and Willis warned me not to trust her.

After saying, "Get your shit," she reached over on the nightstand, rummaging really quickly looking for my wallet. I reached for my sweats that were in the chair next to the nightstand.

She told me, "No, you can leave those here, you're leaving now!" She expected me to leave in my underwear, with kids in bed.

At that point she leaned back over on her side of the bed, grabbed the cordless phone, and threatened to call the cops. I was petrified because of the restraining order. I knew if the cops came I would be arrested and my job would be on the line. Sheer terror went through me. So, as soon as she mentioned cops, I jumped up in my underwear and ran into the bathroom.

She said, "You're not going anywhere." Then she jumped up, with the phone in hand and ran out of the bedroom to the front expecting to grab my keys, trying to trap me in the house.

I ran to the bathroom and stuffed my wallet and keys in the front of my underwear. When I attempted to leave the room, she leapt onto my back, clawing and reaching into my underwear. I didn't want to hurt her, and tried to avoid contact especially since she was pregnant. I grabbed her off of me, trying to get out of the house. She was screaming like a banshee, purposely trying to wake up my step sons to have them call the cops. Our children, who were three and one were crying, hearing the noise.

She was running through the house with only g-string panties on. The lights came on and there stood her boys, 11 and 9 years old, who told me not to hurt their mother and to leave her alone as I made my way out of the bedroom. She followed me and then ran past me, blocking the front door, trying to prevent me from leaving the house. I was trying to avoid any more conflict. I just wanted to leave. It was a terrible situation that none of the children should have seen. I moved her away from the door and ran out to my truck, with cell phone in hand, wearing only my underwear and without shoes. I knew that if anything jumped off, as long as I had my wallet I could get what I needed between cash and credit cards.

TO HELL AND BACK

I jumped in my truck and locked the doors. She ran outside, pulled on the door, but couldn't get it open. I started driving off. I was petrified, just thinking that I couldn't afford to go to jail or lose my job. I didn't realize her position, holding onto the tailgate of the truck. I pulled out of the driveway and she jumped off of my truck after a block, which is when I saw her. I'm so glad I didn't hurt her.

I was on the highway, driving to Willis' house, almost an hour away. It was freezing cold. I was in the rain with nothing but my underwear, my wallet, my cell phone, my keys and my truck. I decided not to stay in Tucson and go to a hotel, afraid there would be an APB out. Driving to Willis' in another township seemed to be the safest thing to do. He wasn't there when I arrived. I called him. He was at work in Tucson. He told me he would be there in a minute to let me in. I slept in the cold truck in my underwear. About an hour later he showed up to his house, and let me in. He gave me a shirt, pants, socks, shoes and a jacket, then he made me breakfast. That's my brother right there!

He knew I was upset, that's why he fed me and talked with me. I then realized, about 7 a.m. that my check was going to go into my account that morning in Tucson. I had not closed the account, therefore she had full access to the money, just like I did. I knew that if she beat me to the bank she would take every cent and I would not have any money for food, gas or surviving. I told Willis what I was thinking.

He said, "Let's go! We're going to Tucson to get your money."

I didn't want to go but he talked me into it. He drove my truck instead of me just in case we were stopped. If I was going to get arrested I wanted him to keep my truck, that was my thinking. The bank opened at 8 a.m. We pulled up at 7:50. Guess who was sitting on the parking lot with Joseph and Angelina strapped into their car seats?

It was payday Friday morning and there was a line of people outside of the bank, waiting for it to open. Frances glared at me the moment she saw us pull up. She immediately threw her car in park, left the kids in the car, jumped out, and ran to the front door of the bank past everyone. She began screaming loudly, banging on the glass door trying to get the attention of the security guard who was inside, preparing to open the bank. As she was banging, I saw her speaking to him through the slightly opened door, while she was pointing to me and my truck.

After we saw what she was doing, Willis peeled off and we left the parking lot. I thought we were heading back to his house but he said, "No Rob, we're heading to another branch, up the street."

At that point I was even more petrified.

"Don't worry about it; we are going to make it to the other branch in time." Willis assured me.

There were at least 20 people in line as we pulled up. The doors opened. I bolted past everyone; I verbalized my dilemma to everyone in line, as I moved past them. Ironically most of the customers were men that morning.

TO HELL AND BACK   29

I said, "Fellas, I have an ex-wife that's down the street standing in line trying to beat me to my account to empty it. Would you mind if I stepped in front of all of you?"

None of them objected. I was the first person to be served. A girl asked my name in a slow and methodical voice. I went off on a rant with my name, checking account and social security number, as I placed my ID on the counter, expressing my urgency. The girl seemed to sense the importance and began typing.

She said, "Someone's in your checking account right now, how much do you want?"

I said, "Empty it."

She pressed the button, asked me how I wanted it, and I said, "Just give it to me." The saving grace was that I had money in both a savings and a checking account, and I was able to get the majority of the money out before she took it.

As I walked out of the bank, the men in line were yelling, giving me high fives and hugs, acting as an entourage, cheering me on. Good ole' Willis had been standing watch and telling them the gory details as I was praying internally and fighting for my hard-earned cash. I had a few thousand dollars in hand when I exited.

At that point, I knew the fallout was going to be bad. She would be even more pissed since I got the money. Everything I owned was in the house and I was afraid she would burn it down, just to spite me. I knew she had to be at work, that the kids should be at the babysitter, and figured she wouldn't expect me to go to the house after the money incident. That influenced my decision to go there as quickly as I could to retrieve what we could get into the truck.

When Willis and I pulled up, we saw the $6,000 worth of Italian marble, which was to be used to replace the kitchen counter tops smashed into pieces in the front yard. That was such a foolish choice. In her rage she destroyed it, instead of selling it and recouping it for the value. I'm not even sure how she managed to do that. I was pissed, but my fear of another confrontation had me focused on handling my business. Willis backed my truck up to the front of the house and I got as many of the most important things I could.

Going to the House Was a Tough Choice

I knew if I let an extended period of time go by without getting my belongings, she would destroy them. Between family heirlooms, camping and fishing gear, and my gun collection, I had to roll the dice and hope she didn't pull up. I was scared, but felt I had no choice. In those moments my belongings meant more to me than the possibility of going to jail.

Willis was right by my side, and had my back. It was just one of the many times he would support me during my time of need. I moved in with him again until I was able to retain possession of my home, which took a bit of time.

Being around Willis, listening to his advice, helped me to develop a solid plan. In one of our discussions, he reminded me of that old saying, "Possession is nine-tenths of the law." All parents, and especially fathers, who are going through divorce need to know that each parent has as much right to the children as the other. The person who gets the kids and files for custody will likely be the primary. Once I knew that, I made sure to have the kids and take care of them. It definitely helped me with the case.

Hopefully, you can avoid, interrupt or end some of your challenges by seeing mine, and heeding the suggestions I'm making. *In the previous chapter I mentioned the importance of physical custody, which lays a solid foundation for being awarded the custodial parent. The fight for my kids was a difficult one and something I wouldn't wish on any parent. Many of the things through which my family suffered are tragic, upsetting and are difficult to speak of. Though I'm getting into some of the details, I don't want my children to read this book and feel worse about either of their parents.*

Fighting for My Kids

Because Frances had made threats about leaving the state, I knew it was crucial for me to have a strategic plan to get our children. Each time we spoke on the phone pertaining to finances, bills and groceries for the kids, I verbalized our need to bury the hatchet and fix our relationship at whatever cost, despite me knowing it had reached the point of no return. After a couple of weeks, being separated, she began to let her guard down and allowed me back into the house, once again. She lifted the restraining order first, then I moved back into our home.

I knew, because of her volatile way of thinking, and the explosive encounters we experienced, it was a matter of time before something else happened. I watched, prayed and walked on eggshells daily. In the back of my mind, all I could think of was living in my home with my children, safely and peacefully. Since it was clear we wouldn't be able to accomplish that as a married couple, I had to focus on me and my little babies...

Early One Morning

We had an argument out of the clear blue, which so often happened. That's when she told me, "I'm going to get this house. I'm going to get alimony and child support. I'm moving out of this state. You won't know where we are."

The argument and threats went on for two or three hours. I was beyond stressed and extremely concerned. I wanted to grab the kids and take off with them in my truck. I felt desperate because there was no way I could live without being with my children. I was going to protect them at all costs.

Before grabbing my keys, I called my mom and asked her what I should do. She said, "Don't run with the kids. You need your job. You need security and stability to raise the kids. I don't know what's going to happen, but pray about it. It's going to work out."

I did what my mother suggested and prayed for guidance, patience and safety. About 30 minutes later, a small voice spoke to me, in my heart saying, "This is your chance." She went in the bathroom, slammed the door and locked it. I knew that was my moment.

We had two vehicles. I grabbed her car keys and mine, my wallet, Joseph and Angelina, and walked out of the house. I had to keep the kids safe while I did what I needed to do. Instead of running, I was going to stay and fight. So, I took them to a friend's house, without clothes, diapers or anything. She took them. I went straight to the courthouse, early. I spent the day there figuring out the process, then filling out the paperwork for a restraining order to have the rights to my children and my home.

They told me it was unlikely that I would be able to speak to a judge that day. It was Friday and my chances were slim, but if I was willing to wait until his docket ended, perhaps I could see him at the end of the day. I put in my request and waited.

At 5 p.m. when the clerk told me the judge was officially finished for the day, I was rushed into his chambers where the judge greeted me by saying, "Hurry up."

I told him in detail, as quickly and eloquently as I could, "It's imperative that I have this restraining order for the safety of my children and for me." After many tears while pleading my case, he granted my wishes, which resulted in the restraining order.

I was so thankful to God that it worked out for me. I left the courthouse and went to the gas station around the corner from the house. I called and asked the police to meet me there. They did. Together, we went to the house to escort her from the property.

I sat in my car as instructed, while she got the things she could fit in her vehicle. I can't get the picture of her leaving out of my head with two garbage bags and the older boys, at seven months pregnant. She said to the officers, "Where are my babies?"

The officer said, "Ma'am, he has as much right to the kids as you do so, you'll have to go through the courts to attempt to get custody. In the meantime, you have to go."

I told her the kids were safe. The fear and anger in her eyes were the saddest thing I had seen in my life. It was one of the hardest things I've ever had to do. She got in and drove away with tears in her eyes. It just about killed me, however I'd do it again to protect my children.

Our Newborn Baby Girl

A couple of months later, Frances went into labor with our child. I got a call from one of her relatives telling me this. Hearing that I said, "Thanks for the call, I'm on my way."

Before I could hang up he told me that she had gotten a restraining order against me so that I couldn't be at the hospital. At that moment all I could think of was being there for my newborn.

I took my kids to a babysitter. My buddy drove me to the hospital in my truck in case I got arrested. I gave him my keys and wallet, and went inside.

There she was, our baby Ruby, alone peacefully in a room by herself. She had already passed from a heart defect, which had been discovered before her birth. I kind of think Frances was expecting me.

I held Ruby. I knew it would be the only time I would see her. She looked tired. A little baby, who had experienced so much in the womb looked worn out. On the way back to my truck I cried for our baby, our children, for Frances and for my broken heart.

She had planned a funeral and I wanted to go. My pride told me to go – it was my baby too. But my parents convinced me that nothing good would come out of it. Her family was pissed that I had custody of our children and we both had restraining orders on each other, so it didn't make any sense to put myself, and ultimately my children, in jeopardy by going.

The day of the funeral I prayed and asked God for the strength to keep going. I really loved my family, including my wife, but the pain and trauma was too much to bear. Before I finished, I thanked Him for allowing me to meet my little one, and for keeping her safe, in His arms.

Kids are like tape recorders, *they remember what they've seen and heard - especially dramatic instances between their parents. Remember that when you have a choice to calm down or act in pride when your children are watching.*

Single Dad

*"Grateful that I see my babies every day,
I can't act like it's an easy task to do by myself."*

Though we broke up in 2006 and our divorce was final in 2007, our battle for child custody, child support, therapy, and visitation lasted for over six years. In the beginning she was as enthusiastic about getting the divorce as I was. But after I kept fighting for the children, she started worrying and being on the defense. Things escalated to the point that she told my parents that I would die – she has six brothers and about 20 uncles. My dad got on the phone and threatened her – I think that saved my life. There was a period of time when I had to go to court several times a week and sometimes several times a day, fighting over nonsense. I had to go through the courts because I could never get things accomplished with her directly. Even the smallest things would never work out. As the years wore on I used not only my salary but also a large part of my retirement to pay the attorneys and the children's counselors.

It was difficult being a single dad, especially because I didn't have family in Arizona except my cousin Tyson. He and his brother Tiny were going through transition around the same time Frances and I separated. Tyson, who was like my younger brother moved in to help me with the kids. Soon there after, Tiny, who had been living in California, asked if he and his two children could stay with us while he secured a permanent place to live. Of course, I said yes.

Three grown men and four little children in my house was an experience. Tiny slept on one couch, Tyson slept on another. Joseph had a bunk bed; so one kid was at the bottom and one slept with Joseph. Them being with us helped. It was hard, but we made it together.

Throughout the divorce proceedings, the restraining order against Frances remained in place, which kept her away from me and from the house. However, as the mom, she had as much right to see the kids as I did.

I settled into being the custodial parent. It was hard to balance sleep, work, raising kids and battling in court, I was *Just A Dad Fighting For My Kids*.

Once the divorce was final, I then relinquished the restraining order, but I was still worried about her taking the kids and running off. I didn't allow them to play in the front yard. I carried them in the store, not allowing them to walk around, and I was always aware of our environment, just in case.

Shortly thereafter, I met Becky, who started as one of the children's babysitters. She would become my long-term girlfriend. As we were becoming more serious, she would bring her two daughters, who were a few years older than Joseph and Angelina, to the house to visit. Pretty soon Tiny and Tyson moved into their own homes, but we remained close. With my cousins, Becky, and all of the kids in our lives, the transition to being a full-time single dad wasn't easy but it was certainly less lonely.

Working overnights offers advantages and disadvantages when it comes to raising the children. One of the challenges was making sure the kids were safe and cared for when I was at work. For about six months after Tiny and Tyson left our house, I had a retired couple who would come over and sit with the kids from the time I left for work in the evening until I got home, about 3 a.m. I only paid them $150 a week and they were great with the kids. When they decided to move to the East coast, I had to make other arrangements. That's when Nana, the little Mexican lady (she's about 4'8"), started watching them full-time with Becky as the back-up.

Retaliation

Though Frances had attempted to clean out our bank account, I didn't think to remove her name or simply close it and start again. I had so many things going on, though it should have occurred to me immediately, it didn't. Between juggling jobs, two small kids, lawyers and the pain, I was overwhelmed in every way. Overlooking that would have serious consequences...

My ex had a history and pattern of getting angry and leaving with our children. She would typically take them to her hometown, which was about an hour away. This happened on many occasions and caused a lot of anguish. Finally, I got tired of it. I couldn't take the emotional pain of separation – theirs or my own. I filed for, and got a court order stating that she was no longer allowed to take the kids anywhere without my consent.

Once the kids were in my custody, she worked part-time, and didn't have her checks direct deposited, therefore she had full control of her earnings. I still had direct deposit. In retaliation, she withdrew every dime out of the checking account, driving to five different branches around Tucson, taking the funds. I never would have imagined that she would do that, though I should have. She knew I had the kids and had to feed them. She didn't care. How did I find out about her antics? One night while I was cooking dinner, the lights went out. I didn't understand. I had the basic utilities all set up on automatic withdrawal. When I called the bank, I realized that many payments had been rejected due to insufficient funds. She had been taking the money over time, without me realizing it. I hadn't been checking my statements.

We weren't communicating at that point. She left me destitute. Had I learned my lesson earlier, this wouldn't have happened. In order for me to survive and get back on my feet, I had to get a second job just to catch up on all of the bills. My parents helped with the kids for a few months. Without their presence and support, I don't know how we would have survived.

Co-Parenting Wasn't Working

When the children started to visit their mom every other weekend, they were at the age when they could talk and communicate what was happening during their visits. I began noticing patterns of ongoing issues with the children almost immediately. My kids were not safe. There were black eyes and scratches on faces. Having older brothers rough-housing unsupervised put the younger ones at risk. That explained a lot and was certainly a concern. They were being exposed to unhealthy conversations and were being hurt physically in that house. Because of the visitation agreement, the kids were being forced to go to their mother's, and I couldn't protect them. Immediately before weekend visits, and a couple days after, my son would wet his bed and plead with me not to send him. The bed wetting started and stopped like clockwork. It was too much...

When Joseph was four or five, he mentioned that his mother was taking showers with him. I blew my stack and attempted to talk to her about it. She told me to get my mind out of the gutter. But I told her he was way too old for that. He even told her it made him uncomfortable but she told him to shut up and do as he was told. I went to court about it. They told me that in some cultures that's normal and we can't tell her it's wrong. It was a back and forth between my lawyers and the courts until she discontinued the practice of showering with our son. Yet, as we were fighting that issue, things kept coming up. The lawyer told me to continue documenting everything. To use the therapist's notes to take to the courts to protect the children, as their notes would be more credible than my statements alone.

Joseph had a tonsillectomy a bit after the shower dispute. After the operation he had a bad fever but they allowed me to take him home. I left the kids with Tiny and went on a quick trip to the store to get Pedialyte and a few other items. When I got back, cops were there and Tiny was denying them entry. Though I had told Frances about the procedure, because it was her weekend for visitation, she was insisting on taking our son. He was in bed sleeping and recovering. Since she lived an hour away, it wasn't safe or wise to take him in that condition.

Prior to Joseph being discharged from the hospital, Becky had warned me to get a note from the doctor stating that he wasn't to be moved out of Tucson. I gave the note to the officers and Frances was forced to leave. By this point in our battle, I had a lawyer on retainer. She was putting us through hell and I was tired. I appreciated having Becky as an ally. That was one of the first of many times I would come to count on her for advice and support during the custody battle.

One weekend when Angelina was about three years old, her mother seemed abnormally anxious to get them transferred to me and leave. We had to transfer bags and car seats and such. Right as she got the last of their belongings out of her car, she shut the door, walked around to the driver's side and jumped in before I could question her about a few things. I found it odd so I turned my attention to the kids. Joseph's hair hadn't been combed and he had a scab on the side of his eye, which he said resulted from a rug burn when I asked him. As I looked at Angelina, who had on a little summer dress about mid-thigh, I noticed she had an iron burn on her inner thigh. I know it was an iron burn because the tip of the iron had left a clear impression. She was still very young so Joseph told me that their oldest brother was ironing his school clothes on the living room floor and Angelina sat near the iron and it fell over on her leg.

How could that have happened? On her inner thigh? Through my frustration and rage, I walked into Nana's house (our point of transfer that day), went into the bathroom and cried. All these things were happening to my kids as I was having to battle their mom and the court system. At times the court was as big of an obstacle as my ex. I called their therapist, who instructed me to take photos and then bring them in so he could document it. I did so.

False Accusation

Frances was so set on getting my kids that she was willing to do and say anything. One of the most painful events was the day I got a call telling me that my daughter was in the hospital. Angelina's mom had accused my cousin Tyson of sexual abuse. Instead of her bringing my daughter back to me after her visitation, she took her to the hospital. When I arrived they told me I couldn't see my four-year-old child because of the accusation. When I found out they were preparing to do a rape exam on my daughter, I threatened them with a lawsuit because that would be very intrusive for a baby.

I wasn't going to let her go through that alone. I took off work to be with her while they performed an external vaginal exam and found nothing. Of course they found nothing. My cousin and I grew up like brothers. I trusted him with my life and with the life of my kids. He loved them, cared for them, and would fight anyone or anything to protect them. There was absolutely no indication or validation for her false accusation. Tyson was a big, tough guy who treated my children like his own. He cried that day, so upset about the lie.

I wanted to fight Frances' boyfriend, who was at the hospital with her. Since she was a woman, I couldn't take my rage out on her but I could take it out on him – since he was a man and he allowed it. He knew the seriousness of her actions. It was irresponsible of him to go along with the charade to pacify her desire to hurt me.

The ordeal was so outrageous that I was forced to stay there for a full day partly because Angelina had to give a urine sample but she didn't have to go. She was crying and miserable. She didn't understand why the doctors were touching her and kept saying she was cold and wanted to go home. It was awful. I held her for hours, forcing her to drink water until she finally had a urine sample to give. They examined it, found nothing. I called my lawyer (again). They did an extensive investigation with Joseph, my cousin and I, the males in her life. They closed the investigation with a conclusive, "no abuse" finding.

About Therapy

"Children need an advocate, and sometimes a therapist is the right choice."

At the beginning of 2013 we reached a vicious peak. With repairs needed on my home, things happening to our kids, having counselors' records, and then reporting to the courts, more than 60-70% of my funds were being spent, attempting to get sole and legal custody of my children.

There were so many influences weighing down on us and I was *Just a Dad* trying to make do and do what I felt was best first, for the kids, and then for me.

Therapy

Sending the children to therapy was essential and expensive, but it was the only way I could protect them, support their healing and development, and further my cause to get sole custody. If you are fighting for your kids, having an advocate who is professionally objective and for the well-being of your children is a key component.

I got to the point that every time things would happen, I would immediately call the therapist with each report from the kids so he could hear it from them and document it. He began leaving his schedule open for me because of the severity of the issues, one right after the other. He was nervous for them as well, that's why I think he did that. He was my saving grace.

He would submit his findings to the court, then have to testify. It was a continuous process of therapy, reporting, testifying, and paying for each session and appearance. I still had attorney fees, past and current, in addition to paying for child care and our basic living expenses. Finding the money was difficult to manage but I had no choice. I had to fight for the health and safety of the children at all costs.

*"Looking at my reflection in the mirror, I looked like I had been **To Hell and Back**. I was feeling like a shell of my former self."*

The straw that broke the camel's back was when it was discovered that Frances had driven her oldest son to another boy's house to fight him. *She was arrested for that. Coupled with all of the other evidence and documentation, my lawyer used that to show her incompetence as a parent. Immediately after notifying the court of her arrest I was given sole custody, as the courts were also tired of her shit. It was mortifying.*

One action can affect you for the rest of your life... Thoughts feed into your feelings, feelings dictate your actions and actions dictate results. One of the reasons we continue to have the same results is because of our patterns of behavior. It's a cycle. When we recognize it's not working, that's when we must choose to think, feel and behave differently, especially if we want what's best for our children.

Navigating the Custody Battle

Every argument and disagreement took energy, especially by the time I started fighting for sole custody. It took every ounce and drop of control, gained through emotional fortitude and prayer just to make it. I had to maximize all of my senses without burning out. I was **Just A Dad Fighting For My Kids**. I couldn't do it all by myself, and neither can you. I would have never imagined how difficult things could be but hopefully this chapter will help you with perspective and action steps.

Considerations When Seeking Custody of Your Children

1. Remain encouraged despite the games, pressure, drama and system.
2. Money, proper representation and timing.
3. Maintain what's in the child(ren)'s best interests, possibly professional support for your children/you.
4. Your attitude and what you say to your children about their other parent makes all the difference.

Negative, unhealthy environments affect children, period. If something is going on that's endangering the well-being of your children, and you feel it's best to seek custody, the first thing you need to do is get the child to a therapist so those documents can be used in court. What you (as the parent) thinks, hears and says, means nothing however, documentation presented to a court by a licensed therapist adds legitimacy to your cause, especially if you are fighting for custody.

The stress of dealing with toxic, unhealthy relationships has taken years off of my life. I knew that I had major baggage going into any relationship – and that I needed therapy. However, I used money to get therapy for my children, and at one point, I was paying $50 per session out of pocket, twice a week for my son alone. Financially – I didn't have the resources to pay for their needs and then add my own to the equation. The appointment sand the travel time added up as well. I didn't have the energy – I was exhausted.

Because of the volatile evolution of our relationship, by the time I struggled for custody, my ex was constantly doing and saying things that were damaging to the kids. But the courts were saying I needed more proof. I felt helpless even though I was taking steps to help them cope, while creating a safe home environment. It was a gradual process, getting things worked out took patience, along with the right people guiding me, like my family.

Men who are serious about parenting usually want sanity and fairness – not to be raked over the coals for child support, alimony and spousal support. We want to be able to protect ourselves and to be able to carry on after the divorce/split. Unfortunately, the system is rigged in favor of the mother. Too many times men have a long period of recovery (financially) based on the court's ruling.

Why? Taking a woman's children, that's tough. And if you dare try, some become calculating. She will think about covering her bases and making a situation look better for her because she's mom, and she should. Document everything, get receipts, save receipts, and maintain records faithfully. Women are usually better at this.

Things You Should Know

Possession is 9/10ths of the law. If you have the kids, it's much more difficult for the courts to rip the them away. What I'm not saying is kidnap your kids. What I am saying is establish a pattern of being the primary caretaker where the kids are living with you the majority of the time. Then be the first to file for custody. Document it all! Record keeping is key. You must take the initiative and file first, or you've done it for nothing. Because once the mother files, it gives her an automatic upper hand.

You must be proactive – in the beginning. A father has as many rights as the mother to the children. Until she gets in front of the judge asking for child support, then it's automatically established that she's the primary parent and you are the secondary. At that point you've allowed them to equate a number (the amount you are contributing) to your kids and you are no longer an equal caretaker.

Choose the right lawyer. Not to sound sexist, but to be real and practical, if you are a dad, choose a female lawyer, or a male who has a history of winning child-sole custody cases. Cases going in the father's favor are rare because custody usually goes to mothers. A woman is better, describing to the court, how a father would be better suited for a child if the mother has custody already. In most instances, the female lawyer discussing the child's well-being, and standing for you as a man, is favorable. She will be able to verbalize your positive attributes, and you need someone who is passionate, tenacious and committed. It's difficult to take custody from a mother, especially if she doesn't have documented mental problems or drug problems.

Don't be in denial. Whatever you may have revealed in the past will be used against you so tell your lawyer everything so that you can create a strong offense and defense.

Of course you may have had deep love and respect for the woman who birthed your children, however, if you genuinely feel you would be the best parent and you have the means and the tenacity to fight, don't get distracted by potential setups, tricks and emotional ties. You must put past feelings to the side and focus on what's best for your children.

You may think you know a person and wouldn't suspect they would do certain things but when children are involved, they can get ruthless. Consider those things even though it's easy to get caught up.

Create a Team

I learned that notes and records will lead you to the promise-land. You have to write down and label every single thing. If you can't do it yourself, ask your mom, sister, girlfriend, or someone who you can trust to help you document what is happening, including dates and times. Samples for documentation include: detailed records for any kinds of discrepancies, disagreements, texts, posts – and when you can, include others – witnesses who can validate certain situations, instances or times. It goes a long way.

Create and have a specific group of people who can help you – babysitters, counselors, and coaches, those who will stand for the best interests of your children. It's important because you are going to need a support system. I know beyond a shadow of a doubt that my custody fight would not have been as difficult if my mother and sister had been in the same city. Being isolated and living with limited family support (only my male cousins around) made it more difficult for me and forced me to play all of the roles for my kids. This is not easy when they are little. I had five people who were critical in assisting me in gaining custody. Through the nightly phone calls, they did support me and give me advice, instruction, encouragement and reprimand when needed, to win the fight.

Ideally, communicating with the other parent is what it takes to give children balance and a solid foundation. However, lies, skewed truths, being in the battle, and the pain of it all can take you off track. Keeping what's most important in the forefront – the children are key, no matter what. When it's not possible to handle the difficulties on your own, using attorneys is what you're going to have to do.

You will also need time, money and possibly support with court filings, documents, serving, being served, being in court, communicating with therapists, lawyers, judges and dealing with the system as a whole. I've seen other fathers/friends who have fought and lost the battle or who have gotten fleeced and how that affects them – now and in the future.

Being proactive if you are fighting for custody is the key because child support, custody and childcare affect your ability to save, live and the overall quality of life – for your kids and for you, in the present and in the future.

I want you to be prepared for being a full-time parent as well. It's full of struggles – ones that most mothers deal with on a regular basis. Don't take anything or anyone for granted.

6 Single Parent Struggles

1. (Typical) Maternal Roles – keeping up with medications and doctor appointments, giving baths, cooking healthy meals, buying clothes, while also working outside of the home. These are things dads don't (typically) have to juggle.

2. Creating Some Sense of Normalcy – despite the chaotic nature of break ups, balancing healthy communication between both parents, keeping the children's needs at the forefront.

3. Creating A Support System – having a strong core of trustworthy, responsible people who can serve as babysitters, friends and role models to fill in for one or both parents.

4. Maintaining Openness – allowing children to talk about their feelings about the other parent while being objective about them, even when it's painful or difficult.

5. Full-time Parenting – addressing the needs of children, especially as they age, and dealing with the guilt of not having as much time or energy to spend leisure time, especially when working a full time job.

6. Dating/New Relationships – living a full life while also exposing children to new people can cause confusion, resentment and anger; or bring new, positive dynamics to your family. Take your time in introducing new people, making sure your goals align with theirs in the long run. If you think there is long-term potential, it's important to build and establish relationships between your partner and the children before coming together in a living/marriage situation.

I'm pulling for you to win. If you don't, because the deck is often stacked, don't feel that your efforts are in vain. As your children mature they will appreciate your efforts to fight for their highest good and they will also remember how you treated them and their mother (other parent), even when you have your doubts.

Dating and becoming intimate while parenting is a serious, serious choice. *Everyone's motives are different. Someone can be nice, good and even helpful. That doesn't mean they are "for you" or "for your kids" in the long run. Use caution if you find yourself in the position where kids are involved – your kids or theirs... your choices have ramifications.*

Becky Transformed Our Lives

"Wanting to be loved and cared for is natural, especially when going through hell."

Over Time, As Fees Piled, Other Essentials Suffered

The custody-related expenses were so high, I got behind on my mortgage. Then things started falling apart at the house. I had an old swamp cooler system, a water based system which circulates air and cool water into the home that needed to be switched to a central air conditioning unit. It caused roof damage, which I believed was going to turn into a mold problem. I had major concerns because my daughter has severe allergies. On top of that, all of the windows in the house needed to be replaced. The 100 degree temperatures, which were normal in Tucson, were too hot for my single pane windows, it was hot as hell in the house. It seemed like everything was crumbling, no matter what I did. I knew I had to make some dire changes, and quickly, if we were to survive.

The kids were enrolled in the elementary school near my house. However, my son was kicked out because of something inappropriate he had said to another child. In hindsight, I should have fought the decision to kick him out versus discipline for an inappropriate comment but I was in the middle of so many other battles, I just didn't have the energy or forethought to do so at the time.

Angelina went to Becky's house, which worked out since it was close. She was used to her and was protected from the mold and allergy concerns. I sent Joseph to Nana's house. I split my non-working time being with them, going to court, and sleeping when I could.

As Joseph was aging, his behavior was more difficult to manage. His new school was close to Nana's house and him being there after school was working out pretty well. She treated the kids like a grandmother. Joseph had a great connection with her and did well under her care.

Unprovoked by anything in particular, one afternoon Frances went to Nana's house with the cops and told them that she was hiding the kids from her. It was a lie but the day the cops showed up was the day Nana's family was having a birthday party for her. It was a terrible scene. After the incident, she called and said she couldn't watch the children any longer. The separation was heartbreaking.

Searching for Stability

Children need and deserve nurturing parents who put their best interests first. So many resources and so much energy was going toward fighting over them that they continued to be negatively affected regularly. Peace was a rare commodity in our lives. I was frantically trying to create stability for them while clawing to keep my job and stay afloat. They had been through so much. Losing their babysitters took a toll on them and on me. I was always worried and critiquing people as they came in and left, about my children. After what happened with Nana, and since Angelina had already adjusted to being cared for by Becky, taking Joseph to her house was a natural progression.

With both children being watched by Becky, my kids and her kids were becoming more like siblings. She cared for them well, they enjoyed having a loving woman in their lives, and so did I.

Let me give you a little background...

I met Becky, who was a widow, in 2008 through her boyfriend KD, a friend of mine, when I needed a babysitter for my kids, who were four and two at the time. She had two young daughters who were six and eight. She was an incredible babysitter and took great care of my babies, along with her girls. I think she felt sorry for me, as a single dad struggling to take care of my little ones, especially during times when I didn't have a lot of money or food, considering the separation, pending divorce and legal battles which were depleting my resources.

About a year later KD, who was a known womanizer got caught cheating on her, despite warnings from me and other male friends. A few weeks after they broke up, she hosted a Halloween party for about 50 people. After it was over, at about 2 o'clock in the morning, the guests were gone, and the kids were asleep. She asked me if I would consider dating her. I was on the fence and didn't say yes. However, we hooked up that night. That should have been a warning sign to me. I'm not proud of what I did however, it had been a long while since I felt like a woman genuinely cared about me, and she had given me and the kids' stability. After a few days I said, "Yes." I was all in. My parents were not pleased with my decision but hey, they were in St. Louis and I was in my 30s, trying to take care of my babies and recover from all of the heartache, pain and cruelty of my recent divorce and ongoing custody battle.

When KD found out that we were dating, because he saw my truck parked in her driveway regularly, he did his best to break us up, and nearly succeeded, using a photo of me with another woman, a hook up he introduced me to, to break us up.

Becky stopped watching the kids for a few months because of the photo. I asked Nana if she would consider watching them, temporarily, because we really needed her. She agreed.

About three months after Becky and I broke up, things thawed between us and we started talking a bit. Then she started watching the children again, and ultimately, we rekindled things. We dated for years and had a good relationship, including me with her kids and her with mine.

Becky worked part-time, and the rest of the time, she spent caring for the kids and helping me win my custody battle. She was excellent at record-keeping and kept me organized when it came to court filings, appearances and dealing with the never-ending issues with Frances.

In 2014 my little family moved into Becky's home with her little family, while I was getting my credit together, preparing for marriage. I spent $10,000 on a recreation room sized addition to her house so that space would not be an issue for the children. We were excited about it because my buddy Luis did it for a $15,000 discount. Things were pretty deep at that point. Prior to us moving in, she had convinced me to put the Jeep in her name because I could get a lower interest rate since my credit score was low, based on the fight for the children. Thank goodness, I had my family in my ear, on standby for advice, and the security of my job to fall back on. And the main thing, more than anything else, I had God.

> *"There were things I didn't pay attention to but probably should have. Things were happening a million miles a minute."*

"Don't get caught up just because of a big butt and a pretty smile."

— My dad, Robert Curtis Anderson, Sr.,

The Shift

"Don't put yourself at someone else's mercy if you don't have something you can fall back on. Whatever little you have, hold on to it if you can, it will pay off in the end."

By the time I had been awarded sole custody, we were battle worn and scarred. Contact with their mom was inconsistent and while Becky was a mother figure, she wasn't their mother. Things were especially difficult for and with Joseph, who by that time, had been diagnosed with Attention Deficit Hyperactivity Disorder (ADHD), Attention Deficit Disorder (ADD), and Oppositional Defiant Disorder (ODD). He was also a 10 year old boy, now living with three girls. Working to get out of debt, I continued to work night shifts and overtime whenever I could get it, which was almost always. Tired and worn down, all I could really muster was work and sleep. Everyone wanted and needed more of me, but I didn't have much more of me to give. Everyone was vulnerable, in their own way, and communication became increasingly difficult.

A shift in the relationship between Becky and I occurred as Joseph was acting out; him being difficult to deal with on top of him not being her child seemed to affect the way she treated him, now that we were under the same roof.

Labels

As a parent, I didn't want my son labeled or treated with bias. He was already young and Black, living in Tucson. However, he was highly affected by the volatile dynamics he had witnessed and experienced. Being diagnosed with those disorders meant that he had a special need for focused attention, guidance and plenty of patience.

Joseph had lots of rocky moments at school. We had conference calls with teachers and I had to watch him like a hawk. In addition to those bad things, Joseph got on the honor roll and was accepted onto the wrestling team, which was great. Yet, the tough things continued to happen.

Most have heard of ADHD and ADD. If you aren't familiar with ODD, here's more about it:

> *Some symptoms associated with ODD are being argumentative with adults, easily losing the temper, acting aggressively towards peers, persistently being in trouble at school, being touchy or easily annoyed and refusing to follow an adult's directions or rules. ODD can be present from early childhood to after puberty and is much more common in boys. The causes for ODD vary and can be a mix of psychological, social and biological issues. It*

may be difficult to see the difference between ODD and childhood argumentativeness and moodiness. Treatments include individual and family therapy, and medication may be prescribed for mental health conditions related to ODD. Source: *ShareCare.com*

I love my son. I believe in my son, and no one is going to mistreat my son. When I read the symptoms of ODD as I write, I'm able to be much more objective now about the day to day struggles he was facing, and those our household was facing as well. But, back then, in the midst of our struggles, I was counting on Becky to treat him with the same loving-care she once had. Becky had been around for most of his life; it seemed she knew how to handle him prior to living with him. I felt she had a bias toward him and it was getting worse.

She also treated Angelina less fairly than her girls, and began telling my kids, "I don't have to do this, you have a mother." I was in love with her and was shocked about how she was behaving. Putting in those extra hours had helped me dig out of court-related debt and my credit score was improving. We had begun wedding planning. I had gotten the ring a few years prior. I was optimistic and felt we could work through the little disagreements and such because she had loved and cared for my children for so many years. Yet, something inside of me made me hesitant. The way she was behaving toward the kids and towards me had shifted to controlling, and that didn't sit well.

Moving in Seemed to Make Sense

Becky had spent six months trying to convince me to move into her home. Yet, whenever I spoke to my mother, she cautioned me about doing so. She said, "Keep your house, don't give her all you have."

God bless the child who has his own. In my house I had everything I needed. My house was raggedy, hers was nice. My appliances were older, she had new ones. However, I had my own, and they worked. When we moved in with Becky, I gave away most of my things, including major appliances and duplicate items which she already had. I didn't want to incur other bills by putting them in storage, so I got rid of them. That was a huge mistake, but at the time, it was what I thought I should do.

I stopped paying my mortgage to pay the lawyers. I loved Becky. I was loyal, and liked the benefits of being with her. Looking back, the moment I said "yes" to moving in, it's as if I gave her my power. It was intentional on her part and convenient on mine, especially since I planned to marry her and give my kids a stable home environment with two parents.

Though my kids and I moved into Becky's house, I left Petey, my old bulldog, at my house (which was still available to me during the foreclosure process) and visited every day to feed and walk him. I also slept there occasionally. And once we moved in, I gave her the majority of my checks besides a few dollars in my pocket, to take care of the household expenses, food and whatever the kids needed. I didn't mind at first.

I longed for a successful relationship built on mutual trust. Both of my grandfathers and my dad gave their checks to their wives. Trust wasn't an issue. My mother paid all of the bills, did most of the shopping and so to me, that was the norm and it made me feel good as a man to do the same. So, in certain ways, giving her my check was much easier because she shopped for the kids, did my daughter's hair and allowed me to be a father, a dad and a man. I spent any few extra minutes with our family, between working and sleeping.

Rushing Didn't Work

Moving in revealed some things about Becky, me and our relationship. If we were meant to be together, we would have been together, but moving in under the circumstances wasn't a good decision. If I could go back, I would have taken more time to tie up my loose ends prior to getting involved with Becky in the beginning.

Blending families is extremely difficult, especially when children are young. It's important that adults set boundaries and agree on how to treat and discipline all of the children fairly and equally. It is hard because every parent has a bias toward their own children. Most families have one child which will be more challenging. But you still have to be objective and fair. You have to talk to each of the kids and get a full picture of what happened every single time before blaming or coming to a conclusion. This was a major issue with us.

Even prior to moving in, Becky had a bias against Joseph, which was a red flag but I ignored it. Once we all moved into her house we were subjected to her rules and her way instead of us having mutual understanding and equitable shared space.

In Reflection

I should have refinanced my house or just moved into my own place, like an apartment, as I had originally considered doing. However, I didn't because of the immediate comforts Becky made available to me. I gave her too much control of me and my children's lives. It ended up being too much for her, her kids, my kids, and me. There were some jealousy issues on the part of her kids – she had put in a lot of time going to court with me and my kids over the years. They were never really asked if they would mind us moving in, though we put on the addition to her house. My children, being that they were younger than her children, didn't really have a say based on what I thought was best for them.

"Decisions parents make always affect the kids."

A Gun Down the Throat

"Terror was my first thought. I loved her. I would have died had she done something to herself, as she stood there, aiming the gun."

Becky told me one day that she resented that I had children with my ex-wife, and not her. She wanted to have a baby with me, and I agreed to try. I was never completely honest with my mother about that situation. I knew she didn't really like Becky and Becky didn't really like my family. I thought, maybe if we had a kid together, that could bring our families together. After a year and a half, we found out I had an extremely low sperm count because of my stressful lifestyle. She got on Clomid, a medication commonly used to treat infertility. In her forties, she was a high-risk pregnancy. We did conceive but there were side effects from the medication, which included severe mood swings. We all were subject to them, and it was tough. Her insecurities were starting to show.

Miscarriage

In December 2015, we were contemplating telling the kids for Christmas that Becky was pregnant. She wanted to get past the first trimester before we told our families. She was right, not to mention the pregnancy since she miscarried.

One night, a couple months after the miscarriage, we had a terrible argument. I didn't want to see her so I went to my house after I got off of work and stayed there. I undressed and got into bed. Around 3 a.m. I heard banging at the front door. When I opened it, Becky was standing there with tears running down her face and a gun pointed down her throat. We had been together over seven years. I remember looking into her eyes. It was as if she didn't know who I was and I damn sure didn't recognize her, I had never seen her look like that. She said, "If you don't want to be with me, then I'll do it."

I did and said everything I could to get the gun from her but she wouldn't relinquish it, nor would she come inside. As we stood there, me trying to reason with her, she finally stopped and said, "Never mind, I'll take care of this."

She bolted to her van and sped out of the driveway. It hit me as I was chasing her that my kids were at her house and were in danger. I ran back inside, grabbed my pants, boots and keys and sped off to catch her. On the way, I called 911 to tell them what was happening. I gave them her address and they told me to stop pursuing, that they had dispatched a car to find her. I ran red lights, going over 100 miles an hour in a 45 mph zone as I told them I couldn't stop because I feared for my children's lives. I was about seven blocks from her house when two patrol cars ran me off the road. They dragged me out of the car, cuffed me and tried to calm me down as I fought them, trying to get to my children. I could have lost my life that night, but I am grateful that the dispatcher had told them the situation, which is why, I believe, they handled me gently, despite my aggression to get to the house.

Instead of going directly to her house, she drove around, and the police caught her a few blocks from her house and arrested her. At that point they helped me get both vehicles to the house and I never said anything to any of the children other than that Becky needed a few days to herself, and that we had an argument. That morning I got the kids ready for school. Later that day she called me, telling me she was being detained for a few days as they did a psych evaluation. She begged me not to tell the kids or her parents what happened. I reluctantly agreed, but that meant I needed to take care of all four of the kids, staying at her house, something I didn't want to do. The doctors found that she was severely depressed and attributed it and her extreme behavior to the fertility medication she was taking.

I felt responsible for her mood swings, since she was taking the medicine to get pregnant. That should have served as a warning sign for us both, yet we proceeded. I was one signature away from moving from Becky's house to a condo next to my cousin's when she begged me not to leave. Everything was good for about a month. Though the level of violence didn't continue, the level of stress did.

Looking back on that night, I'm grateful I didn't catch up with her, as I likely would have run her off the road. All I could think about was saving my babies. Had I caught up with her, I'm sure both of our lives would have been ruined.

Becky remained devastated and suffered from depression. I felt bad. She was getting worse and said, "I hate my life."

I wondered why we were getting married, since that's how she felt. At that point, she started taking out her issues on the rest of my family, people she had good relationships with in the past. One argument lead to another and she couldn't accept anything having to do with my mom, almost as if she was in competition with her. A competition that was clearly in her head...

> *"She gave me an ultimatum, 'It's either me or your family.' That wouldn't work well for her."*

Battles in Our Home

"After my daughter and granddaughter left, the cards were on the table."

Family Dynamics Changed for the Worst When...

The house we shared was pretty big and neatly kept. Becky and I, along with our four children, three dogs and eight cats lived in the ranch style house.

In 2016 my oldest daughter, Allison, brought my three-month-old granddaughter, Malorie, to visit us in Arizona for a week. The visit itself went very well and we all enjoyed meeting the baby and spending time with the both of them. The night before they were scheduled to depart, Allison and I went to Walmart to get a few items for them to take back home. We left Malorie with Becky for her to watch. We were gone for about an hour. When we returned, all seemed well at the house, with all of the kids, including Malorie.

The evening after they arrived back home to Atlanta, Allison called, irate. She asked me if I had seen the photos Becky had posted on Facebook. I said no. She then told me that Becky had posted pictures of the baby with her animals. She was upset because she had made it clear that she didn't want the animals around the baby, something Becky obviously ignored. I began to apologize and told her that I was sure Becky didn't mean it, that I would talk to her, and get to the bottom of it.

Next, I looked at the pictures myself. In one photo, a cat was standing next to Malorie in the baby carrier, on the bed. In another photo, the German shepherd was standing next to Malorie. When I saw them, I understood my daughter's concerns for her new little baby, and also her being upset that her wishes had not been followed – keeping the animals away from Malorie. It was shocking because up to that point everyone in the house had gone out of their way to keep all of the animals away from the baby, including Becky. I was perplexed as to why Becky did that, although I had an idea as to why it happened. What I mean by that is, I didn't play when it came to animals on the bed. However she was much more lenient when I wasn't around. At times they would hop up on the beds and things and get shooed away, likely the animals went close to Malorie, she thought it was cute, and snapped pictures.

I approached Becky about it after my shift and a night's sleep. We did better communicating face to face about serious matters than on the phone. I didn't want anyone's tempers taking precedence over what was most important in this case. That didn't work, talking face to face. Becky immediately became defensive. She began ranting about how we had put Allison up for a week, gave her a car and paid

TO HELL AND BACK

for everything while she was there, and that she was being unappreciativeby complaining. I even tried to understand where Becky was coming from but at the same time get her to recognize what my daughter's point was as well. Becky didn't see what she did as a big deal. I explained that Allison was a grown person and this was her child. Since her actions were blatantly against her wishes, she owed Allison an apology, at the very least. Becky simply refused to acknowledge Allison's position as a new mother and would not take responsibility for disrespecting her wishes. I told her it was a simple misunderstanding and to call Allison. She is one of the most stubborn individuals I've ever known and instead of calling her, she sent her an email.

In the meantime, Allison had already spoken to my mom, her grandmother, and my sister, her aunt. They were all hot. That following night, I had an earful from both of them. They felt the same way – Becky was dogged in her inability to use common sense and was determined to stick to her guns no matter what. By the time the email arrived filled with justifications instead of apologies, it was the third night into this.

Becky said, "Screw her, she is a spoiled, little brat and needs someone to beat her ass."

When she said that I had to check her, "Becky you've crossed the line by making unnecessary comments regarding my daughter. That's my child. You are wrong. That's not what she needs."

Allison said, "I will never go to that house again since she can't respect my wishes."

About a week later I noticed that Becky had gone through the house and took all of my granddaughter's pictures down.

Her justification for doing it was, "Since I can't see the baby and am not going to be in her life, why am I going to have her pictures around my house?"

She went on to make comments about my momma and my sister because they were taking Allison's side. At that moment I became really angry, bitter and knew something was going to have to happen. I didn't know what or how it was going to go down but her position was unacceptable. She wouldn't apologize – which was a simple solution to everything. She purposely chose to attack the three most important women in my life. I was completely perplexed.

As if this wasn't enough, Becky complained about my mom and asked if she could write her. I thought it would be a good opportunity for them to work things out.

An All Out War

I asked to see the email first before she sent it. I read it and told her I thought it was okay to send. Instead of hitting send, she added a couple things before emailing it.

Later that night, my sister called me and said, "Rob, I can't believe you let Becky send that email to Momma."

Momma had sent it to my sister, who then forwarded it to me. I read it and I was furious. It was very disrespectful to my mother. She told her that we had set a wedding date and that my mother was not welcome at our ceremony. We had a big blow up about that. Over the next few weeks, the pots continued to boil. My mother said she would never come back to that house again, and as a matter of fact, she was never going to visit us in Tucson again. I told Becky I couldn't marry her, based on the way she felt and the way she was treating my family. Ostracizing my mom? Thinking she was going to keep her from our wedding?

I never, in a million years would ever think to treat my soon-to-be in-laws like that. I had ended up liking her parents, because in the beginning they didn't care for me. Her father and I had gotten pretty close after we had a little talk one day. At first we didn't see eye-to-eye about comments her parents had made about Joseph, but after that talk, we had an understanding, and mutual respect. That made things easier all the way around. So, to see her behaving this way after that simply stumped me.

Becky was controlling and I allowed it. The desire to control me was always there and I didn't see it. It festered over time. Then it was exacerbated as time went on. She was angry that I wouldn't combine our finances and put our money in the same account. I told her that I couldn't and wouldn't do that until we were married. She then convinced me to get onto her phone plan. After which, she promptly began monitoring my phone calls. If I could go back, I would have kept my house and my phone.

I gave her my Facebook password and she went through my account and reviewed all of my messages with friends. If I was hiding something, I wouldn't have given her that information in the first place. She had a trust issue.

After a couple bad blow-ups she would use her womanly wiles to get back in my good graces. There were so many times when I should have been paying attention.

Becky was skilled in battle. I have a hard time staying on track in the middle of an argument – responding to about the 4th or 5th thing brought up, as opposed to sticking to the initial issue. She would try and make me feel bad because I would forget some of the things I did. I worked hard, long hours and was tired. She often manipulated the access and liberties I gave her. In those arguments, she was quick. She would list quickly what she wanted to assault me with and then I would shut down, going numb to it, calming down until another time.

She challenged me regarding things I felt were my call to make. She didn't seem to have the ability to differentiate between her place and my place, and where she stood with me, as her guy. Most women know there are certain boundaries. She didn't have a filter – she would threaten the kids and me – her words were extreme – she lacked the ability to maintain her emotions, and spewed whatever anger she had in the moment.

She crossed lines. Whether it was privilege or something else, threatening us, telling us to leave the house, it was too much.

The Struggle Between My Lady and My Family

I feel like Becky didn't love me as much as I loved her, she couldn't have. When I look back at the text messages, I see how toxic our relationship was. I physically got exhausted. It took the breath out of me. I felt my blood pressure going up. The relentless negativity. To try and soothe my sense of hopelessness, she would send a very sweet text, or a sexy photo, which eased the tension for a moment. Then, back to a level 10 again.

She would call me four or five times in a shift in order to argue about something to do with the kids, as I was driving down the highway in the middle of the night, stressed, breathing hard and losing focus on what I was doing. It got to the point where I told her not to call at all if it wasn't an emergency. I ended up turning off my phone a few times just to make it through my shift.

Issues with homework, chores and showers were the source of stress as we looked at grades daily, ups and downs, missed assignments, if teachers had complaints. Joseph talked back to her, he walked out of class, dismissed authority and he didn't get along with her oldest daughter at all. Becky would jump all over Joseph, without talking to the other kids to see who was at fault. Her resentment toward him caused her to single him out many times. She would go from 0 to 60, calling me, almost in tears. I would tell her to put him in his room and I would call him later.

The End was Here

I had come to the conclusion that things would get better closer to the wedding. But things kept going downhill. I believe God was showing me in a multitude of ways that us being together wasn't going to work. This included Becky grabbing my children by their necks. The straw that broke the camel's back was the third time she told me to leave, with the kids. That was it and I knew we were over. I knew if she found out I was going to leave, she would have thrown us out on the spot. That would have placed the children and me in a situation. Therefore, I had to strategically plan to leave, and that I did. Unfortunately, I had to act as if things were okay as I got my affairs in order, so that I could leave on my terms and not hers.

"In past breakups I had been immature and emotional. With each experience, I learned to do better. This time, with Becky, I was going to be strategic. I was older and I had too much at stake."

Underlying many of the dynamics between Becky and me, though I didn't recognize it at the time was the Black and white issue. **She's a white woman and I'm a Black man in America.** *Race became a bigger issue. She began lashing out at me in ways that superseded anything a woman would normally do. I have to take responsibility for my choices to date and be in relationship with these women, and ultimately for the outcomes. As a man, and as a Black man, I've learned and will not repeat some of those major mistakes.*

"Abuse isn't always physical."

– My cousin, Jimmie Chamberlain

Fleeing Tucson

"It's necessary to separate your heart from your head. You can't get them mixed up or you won't be able to see things for what they are."

I knew I had to leave Tucson but that didn't mean I wanted to do so. I pulled over in my tractor trailer and sobbed, talking myself into leaving – I had to. This happened a couple of times before I took action to get to my family, where I would have unconditional love and support. Something told me to check St. Louis and see about a job. "I'm calling to see if there will be any tractor trailer positions in the next 2 or 3 weeks; I'm thinking of moving back to St. Louis."

The person who answered the phone was Mike, who said, "I was your mother's manager." This was a call at 12 a.m. when no supervisor should have been available. He told me he would look into it for me. Then, just as I was about to hang up he said, "I had a guy to quit yesterday, do you want the position? If you do, I will send you an offer letter this week."

In disbelief I said, "Yes," knowing that this was a call that had to have been destined to happen. He loved my momma. She had been a treasure to the FedEx team in St. Louis... I was grateful to her and to God for this chance to save my family because I had been praying for a sign. After the call I had to plot and strategize... *God, I'm giving it to you.*

That week, as promised, I got the offer letter, signed it, and turned it in. Two weeks passed and Mike hadn't gotten the letter. He called and asked if I still wanted the job. I realized there had been a paperwork miscommunication and I told him yes. I'm not sure what happened to it but he didn't give up on me. I had been wondering why I hadn't heard from him and he had been wondering the same thing. Come to find out, my departing manager forgot to mail the contract to my receiving manager.

Each day during the wait, the tension had been getting tougher and tougher for each of us. I was also struggling with the love I felt and the inner knowing I had, which were at odds with each other. I was teetering on the edge, walking a thin line when Becky grabbed my daughter and held her by her neck. My son also told me he felt like he didn't want to live, because he couldn't take the way he was being ripped apart by Becky. We were in danger. Something terrible and more serious was going to happen if we didn't get out.

Three weeks prior to our departure I had rented a storage unit at the U-Haul facility closest to the home we shared. I had begun to store empty boxes in my unit, dropping them off every other night. At that point I wasn't blaming. I was desperate to save my children from more pain based on my choices. The whole time she said she could tell I was distant.

Faith Kept Me Going

I was forced to step out of my norm. I had to put my faith completely on the line with God. I had to. My daughter Allison, my mom and my sister were all in my ear, offering to come out and pack my stuff for me. Or to kill me if I changed my mind, which I briefly considered because of the love I felt for Becky and the girls. I told them no. Though having them there could have been helpful, I couldn't risk putting more family members in face to face communication with Becky. Things would have been more explosive. I knew enough to know that however, I didn't know what else to do. I was in the middle, praying and praying. I was forced to walk completely on faith.

Everything opened up. I got tax money I wasn't expecting. I got confirmation that I had the job, and had to report almost immediately. Less than a month after that phone call to St. Louis, I left Tucson...

Moving Day

The morning of May 26, 2017, after Becky left for work and the kids were at school, my cousins Tyson, Tiny and I rushed to U-Haul, got the biggest truck they had, put all of the empty boxes into the truck and rushed to the house to pack all of our possessions. We didn't have much time and did our best to be finished before her return.

Around 1:30 p.m. when she got home, we weren't done packing. I told Becky we were moving into an apartment in Tucson because I knew she would lie and tell the police that I had her things versus mine if she realized we were leaving the state.

She started tearing up stuff, breaking glass and whispered in my ear, "Rob, I'm going to get you. I'm going to hurt myself and blame you for it. I'm going to see to it that your kids are taken from you."

It took about an hour for the police to arrive. In the meantime, my cousins and I sat at the entrance of the doorway and listened to her destroy my things. She ripped pictures off of the walls, ones of our children together throughout the years. She made 20 to 30 trips past us, with broken things she had destroyed from inside the house, things we had purchased, throwing them in the city trash bins. She was crying and enraged, acting out and doing her best to hurt me and thwart my plans to leave. Despite the things she was doing, it was tearing me up, seeing the pain she was experiencing. It was a terrible situation, sad and dangerous. As much as I loved her, with every passing minute, things were getting more and more tense. She berated each of us with every trip. I refused to go inside the house alone with her so she couldn't accuse me of hurting her, a Black man of harming a white woman in Tucson, Arizona.

She called two girlfriends and her mother, who each arrived around the time the police did. When they arrived they asked what was going on and I explained that I was moving out but I didn't feel safe going into the house because of her threats against me. They stood there the entire time and watched, as she lied about items which were mine and the kids – including the $1,000 full-sized mattress, my son's mattress, the Xbox and TVs. She even broke his "Walking Dead" model set, the whole town, shattering three entire sections.

My plan had been to be packed before the kids got home but with the drama, we were not. As each of our children arrived home from school, things got more intense. Her oldest daughter, Cindy, who was 17 at the time, pulled into the driveway in her car. She walked into the house, saw all that was going on and immediately left the house, retreating to a friend's place, something she often did when her mother and I got into arguments.

One of the kids in the neighborhood had gotten word to Joseph that the cops were in front of our house. He had run home, leaving his sister to pick up the rear, worried for my safety. He arrived in the driveway, breathless and sweating profusely, looking for me. From inside the U-Haul I heard his footsteps pounding the pavement as he approached. I stepped out and hugged him, assuring him that everything was okay. I told him to stay next to me, explaining that Becky and her people were there, in addition to the police.

Angelina, 12, and then Chelsey, 14, arrived, at almost the same time. Becky and her mom began speaking to Chelsey in the dining room and then sent her to "keep watch on the jewelry" in Becky's bedroom. Angelina was surprisingly calm, gave me a hug and then immediately went to pack the rest of her things, following my instructions to a tee. I could tell it was bothering her, however she handled it with flying colors, considering.

Every time Joseph would bring something out, Becky would make him put it down and look through it…

The ladies kept watch, with her mother in the living room, glaring at me with bone-chilling cold eyes each time I passed.

It was 7 p.m. when we finished packing and were getting ready to leave the driveway. I thanked both of the police officers and shook their hands. I was grateful for them being fair to me, considering the fact that it was Becky's house and that she was the one with all the cards. I think they could tell I was in a bad situation and that I was trying to protect my children. As men, I think they sensed that.

At the Storage Unit

I still had a few possessions in the Jeep but I also knew I wasn't going to be able to take the vehicle with me. After the packing was complete, Tiny said goodbye since he had to get back to his children. The kids and I, along with Tyson, arrived at the Jeep, which was parked at the U-Haul facility, about 15 minutes later she pulled up. A neighbor brought her to get the vehicle.

I had Joseph stand right by me, helping me get the last remnants of our things out. Since he didn't move, she leaned into my son's face and said, "Fuck off!" to my 13 year old.

I said, "Fuck you, you b*tch, you don't talk to him that way!"

In that moment I felt myself change, as if I was turning into a wild animal protecting my child. As if the earlier, damaging comments from her mouth weren't enough, this direct comment to my son took me to a place I had recently started going with her.

The mounted frustration and anger was changing me, confirming we had to be over and that my decision to leave was the right thing to do. With all of my possessions in hand and my family safely in the cab of the U-Haul, Becky pulled off in the Jeep.

I shook the neighbor's hand. He wished me luck and said how sorry he was to see all of this, as he was friends with both of us. I said goodbye as we parted ways.

The Long Drive Began

We dropped Tyson off at his house. I had planned to go to a local hotel to sleep before hitting the road as I had slept less than three hours in the last 24, however, my kids wanted to get directly on the highway. They were scared, hurt and were ready to leave Tucson. There's more than 1450 miles between Tucson and St. Louis. I stopped at a gas station, got an energy drink and drove 150 miles before I stopped again to refuel. At that next gas station I went in the bathroom and cried. I cried because I was sad but also because I was happy. I yelled. I thanked God because I knew He was telling me to leave although I was ridiculously in love with her.

I got back in the truck and kept driving until 5 a.m., on prayers and adrenalin. It wasn't the safest choice but since I drive for a living, I was able to keep going.

While I was driving, she was blowing my phone up. I didn't answer her calls. I could not and would not speak to her again.

When my mother saw us, her little raggedy family, arrive in St. Louis after that tumultuous time and trip, she said, "Rob, you have no idea how much I've prayed for you. I've prayed for you for years that everything would get better with you and that woman. Or that you would be able to walk away."

In her arms, under God's grace, I knew we were safe.

"If it wasn't for my mother and my sister's prayers, I probably wouldn't be here."

Manning Up

Love and Reality

When people who love each other, how can they not work? It takes more than love. It takes admission, perseverance and God. If you don't admit and acknowledge your role, you can never have a healthy relationship in the future.

Looking back on things I did and said, I felt bad about them because I had done them and they are out of character for me. I started allowing (their) actions to dictate my own. That's when you know you need to make changes because if you don't, you're more likely to do things out of anger, pain, and revenge. I saw some signs, but I stayed because of being able to come home every night to a hot dinner, a warm woman and knowing I could relax because things were taken care of. I rushed in and then stayed too long.

I came to the realization with both Frances and Becky – it was either going to be my health, the law or my kids.

Pretty Was More Important than Patience

Pretty was important to me – I knew I always wanted to be married and to have a good size family, ideally four to six kids. As a young teenager I prayed to meet someone I could be with always and forever. That's kind of why I went through so much in these toxic relationships. They each were good women in their own way. However, I never waited to really get to know them. I liked them and boom we were together. I didn't take my time getting into the relationships. Taking time and waiting comes with maturity. It's necessary to assess what's good instead of what looks good or feels good.

I wasn't putting the time in necessary to see if that person had the attributes I needed. Honest reflection forces me to acknowledge certain things and to see a pattern. I do regret the pain I've caused, due to my immaturity and selfishness. By not doing that, I created some painful, life-long lessons, for us and the children.

Some of the most difficult hardships bring about some of our best blessings. I had to be in some of those situations to bring about my children (the fruit of the hardships).

Responsible and Real Mantras

1. Regardless of the emotional sacrifice, my relationship with my ex will never change.

2. S/he can only affect me if I allow her/him to.

3. Because we have children together, despite our past relationship, I will always have a spiritual bond with her/him. Regardless of what I think about her/him, I wish her/him well and pray for them daily, as my kids are part of her/him.

TO HELL AND BACK

Being a dad to my children forced me to live a certain life – instead of having plenty of women and money, God forced me to put my family first. He knows what He's doing.

As A Mature Man

In my maturity I'm more cautious about women and relationships. I have to be because the kind of pain I've gone through has taken years off of my life. I know that in my heart and my soul. I can't and won't go through anything like that again. I have to be healthy, available, and effective for those who are part of me, near me and around me in my life. I can't get back the years I've lost – but I can protect the years I have.

Joseph's behavior has improved by leaps and bounds – he is maturing. For the first time in his life he has a relationship with his grandmother, his aunt and cousins. He not only gets love and affection from me, but also from them. Our move made a huge difference. I'm still working on things with him but he's way better. In our new life in St. Louis, we attend church weekly, as a family. It helps us all. Understandably, he has a lot of anger. He's made statements about hating the two women who have mothered him. It crushes me.

I told my son that hate is not the answer, it takes away from your blessings. "You can't do that. Pray for as many people as you can. It's your duty as a Christian. That one prayer you pray may be the one that opens a person's eyes."

I force myself to pray for people through gritted teeth at times, when I think about some of the things which have been done to me. It's not easy but I know it's the right thing to do. I'm also grateful to my mother for her prayers.

Better choices are more critical than ever, with my kids being teenagers, that I'm tactical and meticulous in my decision-making. I have family concerns as my mother ages, and my children and grandchildren grow up.

You've been patient with me, through the stories and experiences. Before ending, I'm going to share what I've learned because I don't want you to go **To Hell and Back** *in your life, if I can help it.*

"My grandfather said, 'Be fierce for your family.'"

Black Family

"We are worthy, significant and beautiful, as a people. Regardless of what happens in society, we must know and remember this in our hearts and in our homes."

Chivalry, honor and respect has been pushed to the wayside. Black families especially have been affected by drugs, jail and such. It saddens and breaks my heart. Our generation is the last of the era of "village dwellers" where family, friends and neighbors alike, guided, protected, nurtured and led our youth. The ones (generations) under us are coming up fatherless, and without their grandfathers, solid men to teach and to act as role models. It's just terrible. Too many mothers are holding down families alone.

That's why I said to myself as a man, as the head of the household, I was not going to let my Black son come up in this society without me. I committed my life to raising him no matter what. And when it came to my daughter, I wanted to give her an idea as to what she should look for in a man – giving her an expectation of what a guy should bring to the table. I knew I wanted her to have the qualities of my mother and sister – and that I would do what I could to give her a solid foundation and then allow them to feed into her whatever else she could get from the women in her life, especially since her mother has chosen not to be a constant.

As a Black man, I've always preferred Black women but moving to Arizona, I didn't realize how difficult it would be to find a Black woman with whom I could have a relationship. The first one I met had kids and couldn't have more – I wanted more. The second was my kid's mom. There weren't a lot of sisters there. I decided to date Becky because even though she wasn't Black, we had a connection. Unfortunately though, deep into our relationship I think the Black/white issue became an issue for her, which affected our relationship.

Liberties were being taken, comments were being made that I don't think otherwise would have been made. And because of that and the fallout that I've experienced from that relationship, I'll never date another white woman in this lifetime, I'm done with that. I'm not willing to deal with the differences. I'm not prepared to put into it what I think is necessary to find out/discover or discuss whatever issues will come about – and there will be issues – it's inevitable. Beliefs, socially, family issues. I tried it, I did it, and it's exhausting.

I've always taken pride in the fact that I don't have a racist bone in my body – I have white friends I love like family members – ones I've known for years. My maternal grandmother had German ancestry and my paternal grandmother was Choctaw, both of whom married my Black grandfathers. So that fact always kept me from having hatred toward whites – as I loved my grandmother more than anything in the world – she was my heart. I had never thought I wouldn't date someone who wasn't Black because of my ancestry, so being with Becky wasn't a big deal for me. But it became a big deal for me when it became a big deal for her.

I was so willing to accept her completely for who she was but she wasn't able to accept me. And she was a lot more judgmental. Because the family you come from is the nucleus for how you become who you are – it's an oxymoron. You can't truly accept a person without accepting their family.

So Black man, Black father, there are a few things I'd hope you consider and remember:

I don't think we as Black people realize our worth, our significant beauty, our contribution and our wealth as a people. We don't realize the depth of our Black roots. It's imperative, no matter who your partner is, that you don't ostracize or not recognize your children's heritage, if they are of mixed race. And, to especially cherish their Blackness because it's been diluted and stereotyped to death. It's up to us as Black men to carry on the richness of who we are – as a race, as a contributing people and as proud, strong, productive, loving, caring leaders, fathers and men.

It's up to us to not just call ourselves heads of the household but be heads of the household. And if circumstances are such that you find yourself not married or no longer with the mother of your children, do whatever you can to father them, to fight for their health and well-being and to live by example.

Communicating with Other Brothers Is Crucial

Passing wisdom to each other is key to making it through fatherhood. We have to pick up the pieces for each other, reach out to other brothers. Support each other. Black men have to talk to each other because we as a group have a plethora of information and knowledge. A person doesn't have to be your father or blood brother, they just need to be brothers who give you advice and support about what you need to do. We have to come together, talk, and give each other bits of information to help each other out. Don't be too proud to talk to another Black man and don't be too proud to ask another Black man.

I Tell My Children

"I am a king. I tell my son, you are a prince. I tell my daughter, you are a princess... You must be respectful of yourself and by doing that, you're going to draw those same types of people to you."

Society has this stereotypical portrait as to what you should or should not be doing and that's ass-backwards. I use myself as an example. I use my hardships and their mother's hardships as an example – but I don't down her. I've made up my mind that whatever it takes, I'm going to raise my kids successfully, if it kills me. It's that important to me.

As much as your former spouse, partner or co-parent may have hurt you in the past, do your best not to down them to your children. Over time, each child will have his or her own experiences which will shape their perspective. Do your best to be positive, even under the most difficult circumstances. They need you to be supportive of the other parent, period. After all, you both have been blessed with the walking, breathing, loving, best parts of each other.

"Be still and know that I am God."

– Psalm 46:10

Environment and Circumstances Shape Children

"Although you may feel broken, lost, helpless or incapable at times, getting to a healthy mental state and seeing the bigger picture is a must. You're not going to have all of the answers, and that's okay. But it's your duty to keep fighting, for you and for your children."

Treating People Well

As a small child my dad was influenced by some pretty treacherous people including Dog Man who gave him a knife to cause harm to a fellow 10 year old at school who was giving him problems. This may seem extreme and it was however, growing up in a very bad area in the city of St. Louis as a child, things were very hard. My dad had an older brother who was really tough on him, who beat him up and bloodied his nose at times, all to make him tough. As he began mastering the game of pool at a young age, he also faced many dangerous people and situations, which was a way of life, living in his neighborhood. This, along with his time in the service, during the Vietnam War, played heavily on who he matured into being as a man. He was tough, and he was a man without boundaries, believing there was nothing he couldn't do once his mind was made up.

My dad forced me to eat with derelicts, literally. As a little boy, tagging along with him, I frequented pool halls and other seedy places meeting drug dealers, prostitutes and other gamblers. They all loved and respected him. He treated all women with kindness and respect – including the ones who were toothless, women of the night, and those without hygiene. He opened doors and referred to them as ma'am. Seeing women treated with dignity certainly influenced me, though I didn't realize how much at the time. He brought hobos and derelicts to our house and insisted that my mother feed them, despite her natural reservations about them sitting on her furniture. There was something about a hot meal and being treated as a man, no matter the circumstance, which helped them to stand a bit taller and built their self-respect/esteem.

Seeing the way my dad treated people taught me to search for the best in everyone. To this day I know I can move anywhere, go anywhere and interact with any group of people, comfortably making associations with folks from all walks of life because of my dad.

Preparing Me to Fight

Though my dad never bloodied my nose in the name of teaching me to be tough, he did threaten to do so if I didn't go back and stand up for myself when two fourth graders, Chris and Lamont, were taunting me in school. Something they began doing in first grade. Fed up, the old school father that he was, stood me up on the toilet seat, so that I was nearly eye to eye with him and told me, "If you don't come back suspended, I'm going to beat your ass myself." He often told me that I smile at people too much, and that I was too nice to people, but I got that from my mom.

That day I was scared of the boys but petrified of my dad's threat. I went to school and fought Lamont. I beat him up, winning the fight, and got suspended. When my parents got to school to pick me up, they had the necessary conversation with the principal, in front of me, admonishing me for my actions. Once we left the building, they both smiled and I knew they were proud of me for defending myself. I was proud of me too, especially because I was safe from the wrath of my dad, and for the confidence boost of knowing I was tough, under perilous circumstances. I made up my mind that those days of being bullied were behind me, and that was the last time I allowed another male to physically taunt me.

The Influence of Sports

Shortly after that, I completed fifth grade. We moved to Salt Lake City where I began boxing, through high school. I actually became very skilled at it and competed in the Golden Gloves. I was naturally athletic and also participated in football, gymnastics and track, with wrestling and boxing being my favorites. Sports developed my confidence as a young man. I know I would have gotten into a lot more trouble if not for participating in those activities because I was a high-energy kid. Focusing on sports and excelling in competition kept me pre-occupied, which was a good thing.

I mentioned earlier that my dad smoked weed all my life. I have attributed part of that habit to the PTSD he experienced as a result of war. I think it was a learned self-medicating practice, one which several of our family members engaged in. My dad never did any of those things in my presence. However, he did stress to my sister and me to stay away from drugs, warning us about the dangers of partaking in them. As an adult while I don't admonish anyone's choices to smoke or drink, I'm always fearful of the gateway/possible effects of any and all drugs, including alcohol and am grateful for witnessing the many actions of my father which made him human and a man.

All my life, he openly discussed the ill-effects of drugs in our family, in our culture, and how they were purposely and systematically used to stunt, control and destroy our culture. He would use examples from his experiences in St. Louis, comparing them to other parts of the country we lived in, knowing that environment plays such a crucial role in development.

Raising My Son

Throughout the worst situations in my life I would stop and ask myself, "What would my dad do?" Because he was such an extremist, it helped me to put myself in that frame of mind and do what I had to do in the most crucial times. Early in my son's life we noticed that he too, was high-energy. Being raised with older brothers influenced his rambunctiousness and three little boys under the age of nine found lots of things to do. They also influenced my baby girl.

My son's oldest brother was a very energetic and intelligent boy who was a natural leader. Unfortunately I wasn't able to spend quality time with him to teach him how to lead and watch over his siblings. The second from the oldest was a momma's boy, who also was a leader. I often worked 10 to 12 hour days and was so busy trying to survive and maintain a tumultuous marriage that I wasn't able to give each of the children what they needed. The escalation of incidents between us as parents was too much and too unhealthy for the family to remain together. Soon after we separated, she filed for divorce. Ultimately, that was best for our family.

When we divorced, I noticed things happening with my two children that showed me they were faltering without my constant presence in the home. During the time when we had joint custody, my daughter, at four years old, began spitting and fighting people. I mentioned my son's bed wetting previously. This lasted for a few years, despite counseling. I chose therapy for them because I knew they needed it, and more of me. I also knew I had to survive for their sake and provide a healthy environment. I had to fight for my children.

I asked myself, *What would my father do in this situation?* I knew the answer was fight! That was when I made the decision to change things. I knew they were going to be ruined if I didn't modify their environment and influences.

Fighting to raise my children, to give them the chance to flourish and find their way was something that I did then, and that's what I've continued to do, to the best of my ability.

Don't Use the Kids to Hurt the Other Parent

"There is a need to be completely transparent when it comes to parenting. Transparency is completely hard, but necessary."

Seeking to Hurt the Other Parent Traumatizes Kids

You chose your child's other parent. It's too late to turn back. Take responsibility for what you chose and for who they are regardless of the circumstances. Too often parents have established patterns of self-interest vs. child-interest, and ultimately that hurts the kids the most.

When Angelina was three years old her mom sent her a birthday card. In the card was a photo of me, all cut up. When my baby saw it, she screamed, traumatized at seeing her daddy that way. What was her mom thinking? She wasn't. She was focused on hurting me. The most painful part of the experience was seeing our little daughter inconsolable.

Mothers

Your actions toward the father can have life-long negative effects if you allow bitterness, hurt or anger to dictate what you say and how you behave toward the father of your children. Your life will be much easier and more enjoyable if you and dad work together, your children will benefit from positive memories/fairness.

I've noticed the severe disconnect my son has with bonding and trusting females/mother figures. Dealing with anger and lack of confidence has been an ongoing issue. Educationally, it's also been a struggle. Unfortunately, I haven't always been able to keep up with knowing what he should know because of lack of time put into him due to our tumultuous marriage and violent relationship. And he has problems expressing feelings appropriately at times.

My son is in high school now and speaks of some of the violent times between his mother and me that he witnessed as a young boy. It makes me feel terrible for any child to have those types of memories embedded in their mind. A lot of stuff which happens between parents should happen outside of the children however, so many things happened in front of them, and so he is able to recall. The truth of that is tragic. Since he's able to vocalize his feelings my hope is that will also allow him closure, acceptance, and the ability to move on, just as it's doing for me.

Dads

You must be completely committed for your child's sake. You must remain consistent, use the system and seek support. Practical things will be hard and yet, your heart needs to remain open while you father your

TO HELL AND BACK

children and give them the best of you. That includes doing things which aren't easy, especially as daughters and sons grow up.

Doing hair isn't easy! Nana did Angelina's hair on school picture days when she was little. I did my best to do my daughter's hair and sometimes it looked okay but other times is was sideways and she looked like a little orphan by the head. The kids were always clean and dressed well however the hair was a different story. She was little so she didn't have an idea of how poorly I could do her hair at the time. I had several mothers offer to style her hair which made me feel good in a sense but also terrible, being that they knew it looked sideways too. I tried my best but knew that picture day was above my skill level. Nana stepped in and used the grease, the brush, the comb and all manner of skills to beautify my child on those special occasions.

At that time we didn't have Facebook and YouTube videos for dads who were struggling to do their daughter's hair.

My daughter is a teenager and my mom and sister help her with her hair now, when she needs it. Yet, having talks about self-esteem, body image, proper dress, maturation, boys and sex with your young daughter? Tough. But as dad, we are the ones who set the pattern, example and expectation. If we don't do it – in the home or not – someone else will. Also, daughters watch how their fathers treat women. What are you showing them?

"Whoever brings ruin on their family will inherit only wind, and the fool will be servant to the wise."

– Proverbs 11:29

My Top 7 Responsibilities When Rearing Children, Especially as a Black Father

1. Their spiritual well-being – attending church weekly as a family has been fundamental, helping us adjust to our new lives.

2. Their mental state – being willing to address questions they have regarding fault/missing mom, life, peer pressure and being leaders, not followers.

3. Teaching them to manage emotions. Giving them the space and ability to be angry or hurt but not to allow that to fester.

4. Their education and life skills – pushing them to excel academically, socially and environmentally. They have been overexposed to things and hopefully they will be able to see problems/red flags with others without having to repeat our parental mistakes.

5. Reminding them of their value and encouraging their self-work, talents and abilities, daily.

6. Forgiveness – encouraging them to forgive and love their mom, maintaining a respectful depiction of her at all costs. Always loving the other parent no matter what.

7. Tenacity – life hasn't been easy or fair but they have made it through despite; and they shall continue to overcome and achieve.

Of course, providing shelter, a safe, clean home and the basics like food and clothing are my responsibilities as well – but I wanted to emphasize some of those things we don't always think about.

Building Healthy Relationships in the Aftermath

I've spent time reminiscing and feeling sad over the things which occurred. I questioned why I did certain things like stay in relationships for so long and putting up with unhealthy habits, confrontations and environments. My heart has felt hurt and broken because of the love that was lost and/or not reciprocated, yet I had to move on.

Moving on is scary, horrifying, actually. I feel responsible for my choices in mates and know that my decisions greatly affected my kids. I've always had the best intentions for my children. I can't continue to cry over spilled milk. Beating myself up over what didn't work doesn't help. I've seen so many fathers feel hopeless. I know the feeling and it's so sad. Fixing what needs to be fixed in the present and making healthier choices in the future is what I, as a responsible father, am choosing to do despite the difficulty. I encourage you to do the same.

About the Future

Looking at photos from the past few months, I feel elated and happy because they show what I've accomplished since I've relocated to St. Louis. We came here with practically nothing. They show me my new beginnings, my grandchildren, children, my mom, sister, niece and my nephew. They remind me that making the move from Tucson back to St. Louis was the best, healthiest choice for my family. We can build on that.

Getting to and maintaining your health – physically, mentally, spiritually and emotionally – is critical and is often neglected by us as men. Don't rebuff support and encouragement from those qualified to assist you. Don't choose to suffer out of ego, shame or embarrassment. We, as Black men, whether uncle, cousin or friend, have a duty to help each other for the sake of our own sanity, and for our children and our culture. We don't do that enough. If we did it more, we would be a lot farther along in combating the injustices we encounter. After all, collectively, we need to make the environment in our homes, and at large safer and healthier for our children and their futures.

Resources for Fathers

American Coalition for Fathers and Children

www.acfc.org

The mission of the American Coalition for Fathers and Children is to create a family law system, legislative system and public awareness which promotes equal rights for all parties affected by divorce and the breakup of a family or establishment of paternity.

Dad's Divorce

www.dadsdivorce.com

Dad's Divorce is a resource site for father looking for information and a support network about divorce and child custody.

The Fathers' Rights Movement

www.fathersrightsmovement.us

The Father's Rights Movement empowers fathers to stand up for their rights and to educate the public and family court system about the importance of fathers in society.

St. Louis Area:

Fathers' Support Center

www.fatherssupportcenter.org

The Fathers' Support Center has a number of programs for men to support one another and to learn the necessary skills for effective parenting, personal, spiritual and emotional development, substance abuse prevention and child abuse and neglect prevention.

Facebook:

Black Fathers

A private group started by a single father raising his sons after divorce who was looking for support from men. The group has been featured on "Good Morning America."

About the Author

Robert Curtis Anderson a devoted dad of three, two of which are teenagers, is an advocate for fathers like him, who want to raise their children. He offers insight and tools appealing to men, especially fathers who are going through divorce, separation or who are simply fighting for the best interests of their child(ren).

When Robert can find the time between raising kids and his 25+ year career with FedEx as a tractor trailer driver, he loves to fish and hunt.

www.ingramcontent.com/pod-product-compliance
Lightning Source LLC
Chambersburg PA
CBHW050436010526
44118CB00013B/1545